REMINISCE

VINTAGE FOREVER

FOOD, FADS & FINDS

24
If you know your oats you'll go for
golden toasted
Cheerios with
power protein*
Cheerios
THE OAT CEREAL RE
General Mills
nourishing cereal grain. Cheerios toasts protein-rich oats to crisp perfection. So you can enjoy a
plus power protein that helps youngsters *grow* strong, and adults *keep going* strong.
77
P99-700
42
56
204

CONTENTS

REMINISCE

ASSOCIATE CREATIVE DIRECTOR: Christina Spalatin
DEPUTY EDITOR: Linda Kast
ART DIRECTOR: Kristen Stecklein
ASSOCIATE EDITOR: Julie Kuczynski
CONTRIBUTING LEAD DESIGNER: Angie Packer
LAYOUT DESIGNERS: Payton Hintz, Samantha Williams
COPY EDITOR: Ann Walter
PRODUCTION ARTIST: Jill Banks
SENIOR RIGHTS ASSOCIATE: Jill Godsey

PICTURED ON FRONT COVER:
Bear on page 181;
TV, Yuri Kevhiev/Alamy Stock Photo;
car, The Advertising Archives/Alamy Stock Photo;
book on page 172;
pitcher, *happyheidi.com/vintageamericanpottery.com*

PICTURED ON BACK COVER:
Man on page 141, Wendy Horton;
valentine on page 189;
Jell-O ad on page 14

ADDITIONAL PHOTO CREDIT:
Did You Know icon, RTRO/Shutterstock

1610 N. 2nd St., Suite 102
Milwaukee, WI 53212-3906

International Standard Book Number: 978-1-61765-915-7
Library of Congress Control Number: Applied for
Component Number: 117300070H

Printed in U.S.A.
1 3 5 7 9 10 8 6 4 2

JUST CLASSIC

The embodiment of a typical 1950s American family is shown picnicking in this vintage advert from Chevrolet. The car itself peeks into the image as though it, too, is part of the family.

THE ADVERTISING ARCHIVES/ALAMY STOCK PHOTO

VINTAGE VIBES

ANTIQUE LOVERS and nostalgic thinkers alike will relish *Vintage Forever: Food, Fads & Finds*, a roundup of all things vintage, including kitchen treasures, beauty and style trends, hot cars, holiday keepsakes and more!

Indulge in photos and stories about cherished collectibles, like comic books, and fashion fads, like the bell-bottom craze. Read up on the history of Pyrex and flower frogs, and laugh at colorful and entertaining advertisements—many that may seem almost unbelievable now.

Fun facts and timelines are sprinkled throughout—for example, look back on the history of the iconic Chevrolet Corvette.

All of this is brought to you by *Reminisce, Reminisce Extra, Country Woman* and *Farm & Ranch Living* magazines. We hope this book sparks memories and conversations among your family and friends.

THE EDITORS OF *REMINISCE* MAGAZINE

HEART OF THE HOME

CHAPTER 1

The kitchen is the spot in the home where family and friends love to gather. It's a place where memories happen over Grandma's tasty pies, heirloom dishware and the many delights shared here.

Apples were key for many of Viola Shipman's (in middle) recipes, including apple butter and applesauce.

The Pies with the 'S'

A grandmother creates lasting inspiration from her kitchen.

BY WADE ROUSE

I spent a lot of time in my childhood in my grandma's country kitchen, tugging at the hem of her ironed white aprons, each embroidered with bright strawberries or pretty flowers.

My tiny grandma and her little kitchen seemed larger than life to me as a child. A vintage stove anchored one side of the room, while her sparkly countertops were topped by a breadbox that held Little Debbies and Wonder bread slices.

But the most prized possession in her kitchen was her recipe box. A brilliant baker, my grandma cherished the burnished wood box jammed with beloved and secret family recipes, organized into different categories—pies, cakes, cookies, breads—and all written in her beautiful slanting cursive.

Her Formica dinette table provided a glamorous backdrop for her glorious fresh fruit pies—blueberry, apple, cherry, strawberry-rhubarb—the golden crusts decorated with a pretty "S" for her last name, Shipman, the only demonstrable sign of pride my grandma ever presented.

Her cookies—oatmeal, chocolate chip and thumbprints filled with homemade jams—were devoured before they even had a chance to cool.

That tiny kitchen was not only where my family gathered every Sunday and holiday, but also where I learned to cook and bake, my grandma teaching me the history of our family through the food she made. Her kitchen wasn't just a

PREVIOUS SPREAD, WOMAN AND OVEN: CHRISTOPHER TOLLAST/ALAMY STOCK PHOTO; FAMILY PHOTOS: COURTESY OF WADE ROUSE

Mark a pie with a letter made from extra dough to pay tribute to someone special in your family.

place to cook; it was the place where she connected our family's past to the present.

Her kitchen is where I shared my life with my grandma, too. After baking, she would always cut two slices of pie, pour a cup of coffee for herself and a glass of milk for me, and we'd sit at her table and talk. We'd mostly discuss what I was going to do when I grew up, how I was going to change the world and see places she never had the chance to see.

"What do you think Paris is like in the spring?" she'd ask. "Send me a postcard when you go."

I was still in college when my grandma hosted her last Thanksgiving. I returned home on break and spent most of my time in the kitchen with her, baking the pies for our family, decorating the tops with that signature "S." When we finished, she cut two slices and poured the coffee and milk, as always.

"Tell me about Chicago," she said, eyes wide, elbows resting on her old glossy Formica table.

Every Thanksgiving, I still make the treasured desserts from grandma's recipe box. And after I finish, I still cut two slices of pie, pour a cup of coffee for her and a glass of milk for myself, take a seat at my own kitchen table, and tell my grandma all about my life.

Every Thanksgiving, I still make the treasured desserts from my grandma's recipe box.

Viola Shipman's kitchen hosted many special moments during Wade's childhood. The bond young Wade shared with his grandmother continued to grow through the years.

Maple-Glazed Apple Pie

Even though we've lived in Florida for years, I still feel like a Vermonter. My parents send us a bushel of Vermont apples each fall, and we try to visit in the spring to do some maple sugaring.

PATRICIA PUTNAM LAKELAND, FL

PREP: 25 min. • **BAKE:** 55 min.
MAKES: 8 servings

- Pastry for double-crust pie (9 in.)
- 6 cups thinly sliced peeled apples, divided
- 1/2 cup sugar
- 1/4 cup packed brown sugar
- 1/2 cup crushed gingersnaps
- 1/2 tsp. ground cinnamon
- 1/2 cup chopped walnuts or pecans
- 1/4 cup butter, melted
- 1/4 cup maple syrup

1. Line a 9-in. pie pan with bottom crust. Place half of the apples in the crust; set aside.

2. In a bowl, combine the sugars, gingersnaps, cinnamon, nuts and butter; sprinkle half over apples in crust. Top with remaining apples and sugar mixture. Roll out the remaining crust to fit top of pie. Cut a few slits in the top and place over apples; seal edges. Cover loosely with foil and bake at 375° for 35 minutes.

3. Meanwhile, bring maple syrup to a gentle boil in a small saucepan. Remove pie from oven; remove foil and brush hot syrup over pie and into vents. Return pie to oven and bake, uncovered, about 20 minutes longer. Serve warm.

SAVE ME A SLICE!

Nothing beats the warmth and aroma of a fresh home-baked pie. Featuring the tried-and-true apple, pumpkin and Dutch chocolate pies, as well as the unconventional "corn pie with meat crust," these ads might inspire you to grab an oven mitt.

1961

What better way to make a tempting pie in the 1960s than with a crust made of meat?

1961

For chocolate lovers everywhere, this ad suggests you "serve the healthful dessert with the happy flavor," Dark 'n' Sweet Pudding.

1971

Pie's favorite topping, Reddi-wip, is hard to beat when it comes to convenience.

1950

There's no excuse for bakers not to pull together a quick apple pie with these pie-sliced apples from Comstock. All you need is a can opener.

Shake It Up

Whether on the table or on display, vintage salt and pepper shakers add a touch of whimsy to your home.

BY JOE KENZ AND SANDY GARRISON

Featuring salt and pepper together at the table is a relatively recent phenomenon. Historically, seasonings were added during cooking—and long a luxury only the affluent could afford. French King Louis XIV is thought to have brought salt and pepper together, preferring his food only lightly seasoned with the two ingredients.

The invention of the shaker is credited to John Mason, of canning jar fame, in the late 1850s. Shakers did not prove very practical until 1911, when Chicago's Morton Salt Co. added magnesium carbonate to keep salt from clumping. Its famous slogan became "When it rains, it pours." In the 1920s, large-scale manufacturing of figural shakers began, including those by the German firm Goebel, best known for Hummel figurines.

During the Depression, glass and ceramic companies searched for new attractive, inexpensive items to sell. Salt and pepper shakers fit the bill, and soon companies were producing them in many novel, colorful forms.

A further boost to the popularity of shakers was the rise of the automobile. Increasingly affordable cars fostered tourism, and shakers became inexpensive souvenirs for travelers to take to the folks back home.

1 CERAMIC CHICKENS

Rooster and hen salt and peppers are popular novelty sets. This vintage ceramic pair is circa 1960. Chickens were all the rage because they were considered very French, in vogue at the time thanks in part to the fame of such tastemakers as Julia Child and Jackie Kennedy.

SHAKERS: SANDY GARRISON; MOLLY: ANNA HELGESON

② THREE FACE PATTERN GLASS

This lovely pair is made from early American pattern glass, also known as pressed or Victorian glass. Matching sets of shakers in this type of glass were manufactured by a number of American firms from approximately 1850 to 1910. George Duncan & Sons introduced the original Three Face pattern in 1878. The tops on these early examples appear to be pewter and, instead of standard round holes, the seasoning flows through star-shaped openings.

③ DEPRESSION GLASS

Ribbed green Depression glass is a 1930s version of pattern glass. These larger "range shakers" often were part of canister sets associated with the iconic Hoosier cabinet. These shakers are missing their original paper labels, while the tops are made of aluminum and show some wear.

④ ORANGES

Anthropomorphic characters are common in novelty shakers, and these oranges are a typical example. They still bear an original price sticker marked "Florida Festival" and were probably made in Japan during the 1960s.

⑤ WOODEN SOUVENIR

Rustic souvenir shakers such as these were made from a variety of woods, often local, and came in many shapes and sizes. These hand-painted, hand-carved coffeepots hail from Corunna, Ontario, Canada, circa 1960.

PASS THE SALT (AND PEPPER)

Shaker collection brings new meaning to "regional seasonings."

Molly Cassidy comes from a long line of what she refers to as "collectors, junkers and thrifters," inheriting the collecting gene from her parents and grandparents.

Among other things, the North Carolina public health nurse gathers sea glass and vintage barware, but an assortment of salt and pepper shakers is Molly's largest collection by far. It began when she left for college in Arizona, with a gift from her dad—a vintage set adorned with some of the major landmarks of her new home state. The following summer, she found two more sets at a yard sale. One was from Texas, the other from Nevada.

"At that point," Molly says, "I had three sets. So I thought, *it's official. This is a collection.*"

There's one major rule—each pair must be inscribed with the name of a specific place—so while antique shops teem with salt and pepper shakers, the ones that fit Molly's criteria are a little harder to come by. But, she says, "a big part of collecting is the hunt."

The most unusual sets are among her very favorites, including one with a curious characterization of Florida: a tiny toaster with two removable slices of toast, one holding salt and the other pepper. "For some reason, Florida is being represented with toast and toasters," she says. "It makes no sense."

Now with about 75 sets, Molly's collection has a few duplicate states but no duplicate styles. Not every state is accounted for yet, but she's working on it.

YOU HAD ME AT JELL-O

Gelatin desserts have been popular in the United States since Thomas Jefferson's banquets at Monticello, and their appeal endures today.

1922

In a time before healthier options like sugar-free Jell-O, the company urged parents to let kids indulge in the syrupy snack.

1963

As adding vitamin supplements to food products became a widely used tactic to boost sales, Royal first added vitamin C to its gelatin desserts in 1955.

1936

In contrast to the "imitation" flavors of some brands, real raspberries—"35 to 50 of them" per package, in fact—were touted in this Royal promotion.

NEW! NEW! NEW!
For deep, dark and delicious desserts

BLACK CHERRY

BLACK RASPBERRY

GRAPE

3 NEW JELL-O FLAVORS

JELL-O New! IMITATION BLACK CHERRY FLAVOR

New JELL-O IMITATION BLACK RASPBERRY FLAVOR

JELL-O NEW IMITATION GRAPE FLAVOR

We've captured three wonderful *new* flavors to bring a new kind of dessert variety to your table!

They're deep, dark and delicious delights that imitate to perfection the exciting taste of sun-ripened black raspberries, the darkest, juiciest cherries on the tree, and plump, deep-purple Concord grapes.

For extra-colorful, extra-flavorful new desserts, try all three: *Imitation Black Raspberry, Imitation Black Cherry and Imitation Grape flavors.*

JELL-O IS A REGISTERED TRADE-MARK OF GENERAL FOODS CORPORATION

APRIL, 1956

1956

Jell-O takes a hedonistic approach in this ad, promising "deep, dark and delicious desserts" that look as decadent as they do colorful.

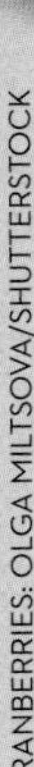

Cranberry Jell-O Salad

This refreshing side dish was a tradition at my grandma's (Ada Miller of Chelan, Washington) holiday table, and thanks to my mom (Doris Miller Craig of Oak Harbor, Washington), four generations have now enjoyed "Grandma's cranberry salad" at Thanksgiving. As part of the last generation to have regularly eaten gelatin-based salads, I'm delighted this recipe is being passed down through our family. The flavor complements any roasted meat.

GAIL CRAIG • MOSES LAKE, WA

PREP: 20 min. + chilling • **MAKES:** 10 servings

- **1 pkg. (12 oz.) fresh cranberries**
- **1 cup sugar**
- **1 apple, unpeeled, quartered, and cored**
- **1 orange, unpeeled and quartered**
- **1 can (20 oz.) crushed pineapple, drained**
- **1 pkg. (6 oz.) raspberry-, cherry-, or cranberry-flavored gelatin**
- **2 cups boiling water**
- **Mayonnaise, optional**

1. Coarsely grind the cranberries in food processor or blender.
2. Combine sugar and berries in bowl; refrigerate 6-8 hours.
3. Coarsely grind the apple and orange in a food processor or blender. Mix all fruit together; set aside.
4. In separate bowl, dissolve gelatin in boiling water. Combine gelatin and fruit mixture; pour into 6-cup ring mold coated with cooking spray or 2½-qt. serving bowl. Cover and refrigerate until set, 1-2 hours. If desired, serve with a dollop of mayonnaise.

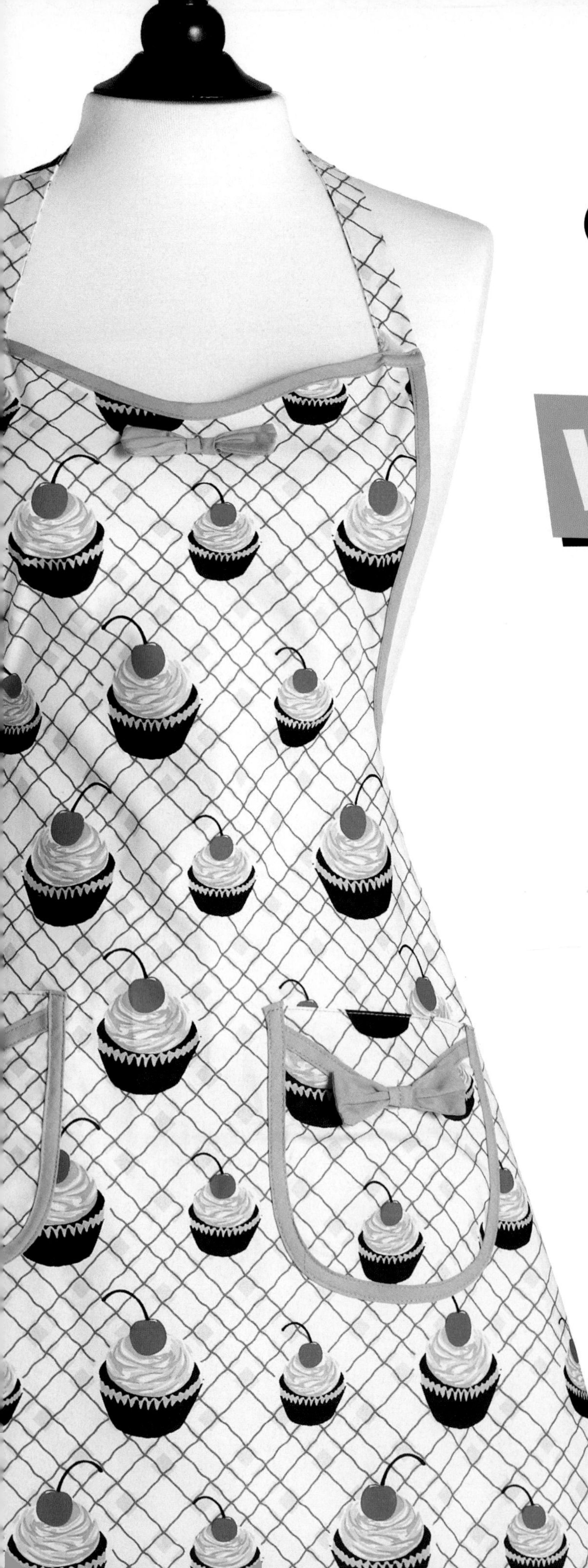

Cute as a Hug

The tug of apron strings returns, stronger than ever.

BY SHARON SELZ

Whatever happened to aprons? If you thought these useful items had been relegated to June Cleaver's closet, think again. Homemakers and career women alike are wearing them as a badge of honor. Aprons are back with sass and attitude.

"I couldn't be more excited to see women tying them on again," says EllynAnne Geisel, author and apron historian. "They've gone from being symbols of domestic drudgery in the '60s to celebrating the spirit of women. Aprons don't hold us back as much as they take us back."

Apron Memories (*apronmemories.com*) is her online homage to aprons, featuring some of the 500 she's collected over the years. It also spotlights photos and warm reminiscences from apron admirers of all ages. "Every apron has a story," she notes.

"Young women are rediscovering their homemaker gene—learning to sew, cook, can and garden. And the revival of aprons has gone along with it."

For others, EllynAnne said, there's an emotional pull toward their mother's and their grandmother's aprons—the colorful gingham, front pockets filled with fresh eggs and the floury smell of muslin on baking day. "When we tie an apron around us, we can almost feel their hugs again," she says.

ICONS OF THE KITCHEN

It's easy to get wrapped up in nostalgia when visiting Carolyn Terry's Apron Museum in Iuka, Mississippi. Her 1,800 examples date back to the Civil War. "Aprons reflect what's going on in our world like a mirror," she says, and her displays trace the evolution of the humble "household uniform."

‹ Fun and fashionable aprons like this one from the Jessie Steele collection are designed to catch eyes as well as splatters and spills.

CUPCAKE APRON: *JESSIESTEELE.COM*; APRON CLOTHESLINE: ELLYNANNE GEISEL, AUTHOR OF *THE APRON BOOK*; CAROLYN: CAROLYN TERRY THE APRON MUSEUM

> When we tie an apron around us, we can almost feel Grandma's hugs again.

"They were functional and basic when we were first settling our country. In the 1920s, art deco prints were in. Feed sacks served as apron fabric during the Depression, and they became wildly fashionable during the '50s, the apron's heyday."

Carolyn credits the popularity of the Food Network, home cooking, crafting and retro fashions for the comeback, and notes, "They've become beautiful again."

Strung along museum walls and pinned to clotheslines are aprons made from calico, canvas, dainty handkerchiefs, organza, leather, recycled denim and more. Frothy party-worthy numbers hang next to workaday aprons worn by blacksmiths, carpenters, storekeepers and housewives.

Carolyn became an apron aficionado with the floral print apron that her grandmother stitched for her when she was 6. Since then, she's found treasures at estate sales and auctions, on eBay and among donations from around the globe. "To my knowledge, this is the only apron museum in the world," Carolyn says. "People everywhere have worn aprons—probably back to cavemen wearing pelts. They're a link that connects us."

Carolyn's collection includes all things apron—from fine art prints and books to greeting cards and old sewing patterns. Visitors' reactions vary. "Baby boomers remember aprons as a part of everyday life, from when they made their first one

Continued on page 18 ▸

Carolyn Terry curates a colorful collection of the humble kitchen cover-ups, dating to the 1860s. Visitors to her ever-expanding museum, which opened in 2006, can find vintage sewing patterns, books, photos and a breathtaking assembly of old and new aprons, some for sale.

in home economics," she says. "To younger women, everything is 'vintage.' They tell me they wish they could have been born in the era of beautiful aprons."

A STYLISH REVIVAL

Historically, for aprons, fashion has taken a bit of a back seat to function. In California, Helena Steele and daughter Claire have a different take with their flirty, figure-flattering brand they describe as "fearlessly feminine." Jessie Steele aprons (*jessiesteele.com*), named for Helena's grandmother, are sold in 32 countries.

"Aprons have to be fun and full of personality," says Claire. "By mixing today's styles with yesterday's prints and designs, we've come up with aprons that are charmingly old-fashioned with a modern twist."

To add to their kitchen couture, Helena and Claire have whipped up coordinating accessories—from oven mitts and rubber gloves to towels and tote bags. "At the turn of the new century, I saw the world trending back to family, community and the comforts of home," Helena says. "I realized it was the perfect time to reintroduce the apron as a positive fashion statement."

If you think the apron's resurgence is a flash in the pan, talk to Glory Albin, a baker and food blogger (*glorioustreats.com*) from Sacramento, California. "When I was planning my daughter Grace's birthday party, I decided to make aprons as favors for her guests," she says. "The girls loved them so much, they kept them on all day.

"Passing aprons along from mother to daughter can be a simple symbol of a heritage shared—like handing down recipes and baking techniques. I hope when my girls are older and put on aprons in their own homes, they'll remember the special times we spent together in the kitchen."

APRONS THROUGH THE AGES

- **The first known reference** to an apron tells of Adam and Eve sewing fig leaves together. (Genesis 3:7)
- **The English word "apron"** came from *naperon*, an old French word for napkin or small tablecloth.
- **Tradesmen in the Middle Ages** were called "apron men," each with their own style of the garment. Gardeners wore blue; butlers, green; cobblers, black.
- **Folklore has it** that if your apron strings come loose, your true love is thinking of you.
- **The pinafore** got its name because it was originally pinned to the front of—afore—a dress.
- **Pioneer women's aprons** had a pocket in back that could hold a rifle, should the wearer need to protect her children and livestock.
- **The gingham apron dress** Judy Garland wore in *The Wizard of Oz* was sold at auction for $480,000.
- **Julia Child's denim aprons** were custom-made to accommodate her 6-foot-plus height.

Julia Child smiles brightly on the set of her TV cooking show, *The French Chef*. She is wearing her classic denim apron.

JULIA CHILD: GERRY NADEL/PENSKE MEDIA/REX/SHUTTERSTOCK

VINTAGE ICON

HERO TOOL, BAKER'S DELIGHT

For 100 years, the KitchenAid stand mixer has whipped up lasting memories.

SINCE ITS LAUNCH IN 1919, the KitchenAid stand mixer has given chefs, bakers and home cooks ample reason to celebrate. With its powerful motor, rotating blade and solid base, it's a trusty workhorse in the kitchen.

Although attachments for the mixer such as knife sharpeners, can openers, silver buffers, vegetable spiralizers, sheet cutters, slicer/shredders, food processors, citrus juicers, etc., have changed over the years, older accessories still fit new models.

Hoisting a stand mixer onto the countertop and plugging it in often opens a floodgate of favorite memories—of baking birthday cakes, anniversary pies, Christmas cookies, Hanukkah doughnuts or Sunday brunch biscuits.

1919

The 65-pound Model H-5, made by the Hobart Manufacturing Co. in Greenville, Ohio, sold in 1919 for $189 ($2,800 in today's dollars). An executive's wife called the appliance "the best kitchen aid I've ever had."

1937

In 1937, Egmont Arens designed the Model K stand mixer, bearing the familiar shape that would eventually get its own trademark and become a kitchen icon.

1950

By the 1950s, home cooks were hungry for innovation, and they devoured any new tool with deluxe features. Appealing to savvy consumers' appetites, KitchenAid touted the stand mixer's full planetary action, as well as its built-in power unit and juicer attachment. Three models were sold at varying price points to appeal to bakers at all skill levels.

1955

Colors—Petal Pink, Island Green, Sunny Yellow, Satin Chrome and Antique Copper—joined white as options for mixers in 1955.

2018

In 2018, the company introduced its first-ever color of the year, Bird of Paradise. Today, KitchenAid stand mixers come in more than 80 colors and finishes.

MIXERS AND AD: KITCHENAID; PAINT SWATCHES: THOMAS BETHGE/SHUTTERSTOCK

Little Rebecca (above) enjoyed helping Mama and Nona (left) make tasty lasagna for their family's big Sunday meal.

LAYERED WITH LOVE

I GREW UP in the kitchen with my mother, Cosmo, and my Grandmother Josephine. As the youngest in the family, with my four siblings starting their own families when I was a kid, I spent much of my childhood helping Mama and Nona prepare flavorful Italian feasts.

In the morning we'd put on our aprons, then head out into the garden to pick the reddest tomatoes you've ever seen, plus homegrown garlic, basil, oregano and spinach. Back then we didn't buy anything from a store except the sausage.

The real magic happened back in the kitchen. Nona began cutting the tomatoes and boiling them down to make her sauce, while Mama chopped the garlic. My job was to get the homemade noodles off the drying rack and bring them to the table where we prepared a big meal for everyone to come home to after Sunday Mass.

While listening to Dean Martin, we layered pan after pan of homemade lasagna, sometimes making as many as six. One or two pans would go to the soup kitchen where Mama and Nona volunteered every Wednesday. When the lasagna was done, we made a delicious wedding soup.

Looking back, I cherish those days in the kitchen. Mama's mind isn't what it used to be, but when she reaches her loving hand out to me, the sounds and aromas of my childhood come flooding back. These days I continue our family tradition by organizing community dinners at our church. I feel blessed for the love and passion for cooking that Mama and Nona instilled in me.

REBECCA BROTHERS • NILES, OH

VINTAGE EATS

UH-OH: SPAGHETTIOS

There are reportedly about 1,750 O's floating around in each 15-ounce can. Who knew?

WHEN MY BROTHERS and I were young, we would stay at the home of a family friend while our parents went out to dinner parties. Those nights, Mama would take us to the A&P to pick out our favorite SpaghettiOs flavor to bring home and prepare for supper. I'm 51 now, and SpaghettiOs with franks are still in my pantry!

SUZANNE SIMMONS

JUST OPENING THE CAN turned us off, but our kids loved SpaghettiOs. They were a great meal for babysitters to feed three kids. When rushed to get to an afternoon soccer game, we couldn't open that can quick enough! Our 50-year-old daughter still loves them. Our three grandsons have been raised on them—must be in their father's genes.

GORDON AND LANE NICHOL

MY LITTLE GIRL, Lori Jo, who is now 52, loved SpaghettiOs when she was a child. They were her absolute favorite! I was a single mom at the time, and I loved that they were so tasty and an easy fix for her lunches.

BARB HARDCASTLE

SPAGHETTIOS WERE A LIFESAVER for me for years. My daughter, Linda, loved SpaghettiOs and never had trouble finishing her dinner anytime I served them. More than once, she wanted them for breakfast.

CLYEDA SIMMONS TEZAK

I NEVER DID believe that spaghetti grew in circles. I still love the straight kind!

JIMMY KAIL

VINTAGE ADS

KITCHENS WITH STYLE

What better place in the home to show off personality and pizazz than where the meals are made? Options abound!

Marlite wall and ceiling panels were desired for their easy-clean, kid-friendly appeal.

A midcentury ad from Youngstown Kitchens boasted steel cabinets, a "Food Waste Disposer" and affordability for families. You don't only see Mom in the kitchen, either, with their beautifully illustrated kitchen ideal.

Enjoy a country kitchen with modern conveniences like a stainless steel sink and "Pop-Up" mixer cabinet, as touted in this ad.

Party with Fiesta Ware

Even now, this colorful dishware still bowls us over.

BY BARBARA J. EASH

The glossy, colorful Fiesta line of china—popularly known as "Fiesta ware"—was born during the Great Depression, aiming to affordably brighten dinner tables and lives. Designed by Frederick Hurten Rhead for the Homer Laughlin China Co. in Newell, West Virginia, it was introduced to the public in 1936 and quickly became a mainstay in kitchens across the country.

The original five Fiesta colors were red, yellow, cobalt blue, light green and ivory; turquoise was added a year later. The beauty of the concept was that pieces could be easily mixed and matched, and bought individually or in small batches instead of costly sets.

Fiesta's streamlined design featured an art deco style with concentric circles that made it look as if it were handmade on a potter's wheel. Of course, the sturdy china was mass-produced, selling at five-and-dimes like Woolworth's and department stores such as Gimbels.

A 24-piece place setting sold for $11 in the 1930s. Today, prices can change as often as monthly, but basic pieces are generally worth less than coffeepots, candleholders, casserole dishes, pitchers or vases. Rarities can cost hundreds of dollars.

GETTING FESTIVE

Early ads for Fiesta were aimed squarely at middle-class housewives. The bold solid colors were welcomed as something radically new, and helped reflect a more

Complete set of vintage Fiesta nesting bowls.

HAPPYHEIDI.COM/VINTAGEAMERICANPOTTERY.COM (3)

WANT TO START COLLECTING?

Barbara, a certified personal property appraiser, recommends two of her resources: *The Collector's Encyclopedia of Fiesta,* by Bob and Sharon Huxford, and the collectors website *happyheidi.com.*

‹ Vintage Fiesta sweets comports in six early colors.

informal lifestyle. An advertising brochure proclaimed, "Color! That's the trend today...It's FUN to set a table with Fiesta!"

As the Fiesta phenomenon grew, the company created new shades to suit changing tastes, making softer pastels in the early 1950s and returning to bright hues in the early '60s. Of all the colors, the original orange-red is valued especially highly by collectors because of its scarcity. The red glaze formula included uranium, essential to the World War II effort and unavailable to potteries for several years.

Fiesta fever cooled steadily from peak sales in 1948, when 30 million pieces were shipped. Earth-toned Fiesta in the late 1960s proved unpopular, and the line was discontinued in 1973. Before long, however, sales on the secondary market began to flourish as baby boomers began collecting, nostalgic for their mothers' and grandmothers' dishware. Rummage sales, eBay and auctions offered a rainbow of vintage Fiesta.

NEW FIESTA FANS

In 1985, Bloomingdale's approached Homer Laughlin about reproducing an updated version in honor of Fiesta's 50th anniversary. It was reintroduced the next year with new clays, colors and glazes.

Modern Fiesta, known as Post 86, is microwave- and dishwasher-safe, as well as ovenproof and lead-free, and both Macy's and Kohl's report it to be by far their best-selling everyday china. To keep the line vibrant, a new color is added annually while others are retired. Shades entering the Fiesta spectrum range from tangerine and plum to peacock and flamingo.

Not only has the iconic china spawned the Homer Laughlin China Collectors Association and an annual convention, it was honored with its very own postage stamp in 2011. What's more, a new generation is celebrating Fiesta. One collector told me, "My 8-year-old is the pickiest of eaters—but she'll even eat leftovers if she can select the color plate her food goes on."

‹ Vintage red Fiesta disk pitcher.

CHAMPIONS OF BREAKFAST

To see these ads tell it, the most important meal of the day is important for any number of reasons: your health, your happiness, or simply your taste buds. Grab a spoon and dig in!

1913

Post Toasties were the Post Foods 1904 answer to Kellogg's cornflakes. Until 1908, Toasties were called Elijah's Manna, outraging religious consumers. This ad trades biblical clout for the simpler promise of a happy, energetic child.

If you know your oats you'll go for
golden toasted
Cheerios with
power protein*

Cheerios

THE OAT CEREAL RE

General Mills

*Nature makes oats the most nourishing cereal grain. Cheerios toasts protein-rich oats to crisp perfection. So you can enjoy a breakfast with all the flavor of toasted oats…plus power protein that helps youngsters *grow* strong, and adults *keep going* strong.

1958

In 1945, Cheerios changed its name from CheeriOats but kept the healthy, golden grains as a vital part of its image. In this ad, a bowl of Cheerios becomes as wholesome as the amber waves of grain it's set against.

VARIETY IS THE SPICE OF LIFE

WHENEVER I WENT to the grocery store with my mom, I would ask for the Kellogg's variety pack of cereals. She always said it was too expensive and would instead buy a big box of Kellogg's Rice Krispies.

One night, I had a sleepover at my friend Janet's house. Her parents took us to a movie, and on the way home, they stopped at the grocery store and asked me what my favorite kind of cereal was. Without hesitation, I blurted out, "Kellogg's variety pack!" And they bought it for me!

All I remember from that night is going to bed with that glorious image of all those tiny little boxes of cereal waiting for me.

I was so excited when I got to the breakfast table. I guess it was just the heady idea of having options that appealed to me—though I'm embarrassed to say that I chose the Rice Krispies.

Whenever I looked back on this incident, it bothered me to think I was so impolite. So about 10 years ago, I wrote a letter to Janet's parents and apologized for being so ill-mannered. They wrote back saying they didn't remember anything about that day but that they'd gotten a good laugh from reading my letter.

LINDA PRICE • GLENDORA, CA

VINTAGE EATS

MASCOTS BY THE SPOONFUL

IN THE CEREAL WORLD of the '50s, '60s and '70s, any mascot could come out on top. Some established creatures, such as the Pink Panther, lasted for only a few years, while simple clowns sold their products for decades. Human characters, including Lovable Truly the postman and King Vitaman, often retired earlier than critters like Sonny the Cuckoo Bird. But there are exceptions; Cap'n Crunch has been steering his ship of cereals since 1963.

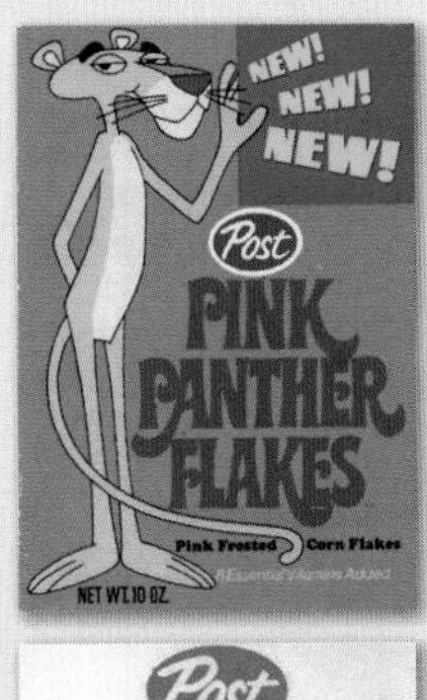

CEREAL: MAYAKOVA/SHUTTERSTOCK; KELLOGG'S AD: COURTESY KELLOGG'S; CEREAL BOX IMAGES: DAN GOODSELL; KABOOM BOX IMAGE: TIM HOLLIS

Pyrex Returns

The patterns from yesteryear are in high demand once again.

BY JOE KENZ AND SANDY GARRISON

The humble beginnings of Pyrex kitchenware, one of today's hottest collectibles, can be traced to a moment in American railroading history. A new kind of glass was needed so that hot lantern globes and battery jars wouldn't crack in cold weather. Corning Glass Works was brought on board to solve the problem, and its work was so successful Corning scientists eventually explored new ways to use the glass. When Corning researcher Jesse Littleton gave his wife, Bessie, a sawed-off battery jar to bake in, Pyrex's future in the kitchen began.

While most Pyrex remains affordable to collect, rare colors or pieces, such as the elusive Lucky in Love casserole dish, can fetch hundreds to thousands of dollars. Here's a sampling:

BUTTERPRINT ROUND CASSEROLE SET

Butterprint was one of the first patterns offered on Pyrex's Cinderella nesting bowls line before it was placed on other sets, such as these casserole dishes. The long-running Butterprint pattern depicts an Amish farmer and his wife holding a bushel of produce, surrounded by roosters, wheat and corn. This popular pattern was produced from 1957 to 1968 and it came in several colors.

PRIMARY COLORS NESTED MIXING BOWLS

Introduced in 1945, the iconic yellow, green, red and blue mixing bowls were the first colored pieces of Pyrex produced, using an overlay on plain white opal ware. The set includes four sizes: 1.5-pint, 1.5-quart, 2.5-quart and 4-quart.

SNOWFLAKE CASSEROLE

Along with Pink Daisy, Snowflake was Pyrex's first screen-printed pattern. Snowflake came in three variations: white on turquoise, turquoise on white, and white on black. The black snowflake dishes (pictured here) were only manufactured from 1956 to 1960, making them the most rare. The lids could be used in a myriad of ways, such as covers, trivets and serving pieces.

DOT BOWLS

One of Pyrex's most popular patterns, called by several names, this design features three bands of colored, connected polka dots circling a white bowl. The first three Dot bowls—orange, yellow and blue—were sold separately. Because of the pattern's popularity, a larger bowl with green dots was added later.

PYREX: SANDY GARRISON

FEAST FOR THE EYES

Collectible chalkware fruit brought color to postwar kitchens.

BY BARBARA J. EASH

NOT THAT LONG AGO, kitchens were utilitarian, with little in the way of decor. But women who spent long hours preparing meals for their families soon found ways to brighten up the space—like hanging inexpensive collectible chalkware fruit on the wall.

World War II had filled the early 1940s with worry, rationing and sacrifice. With the war's end, the nation's mood lifted and budgets eased. Kitchens brightened as women welcomed color to floors and walls.

Remember, even bananas were relatively new and exotic for most Americans then; shipping of fresh produce was limited. People ate fresh fruit only when in season. Colorful apples, grapes, cherries and more became a popular motif on curtains and canisters and in dimensional chalkware wall plaques.

Despite the name, chalkware isn't made of chalk, but molded plaster of Paris painted in brilliant watercolors or occasionally oils. It was often molded into lightweight figurines, too.

Inexpensive chalkware was often given away at carnivals and sold in gift shops as souvenirs. Honeymooners might bring home a fruit plaque bearing a Niagara Falls decal or stamp.

Two-inch fruit pieces sold for as little as 16 cents, a 14-inch plaque with several fruits for $1.50. Some pieces had hooks on the bottom to hang potholders, while others held string. Fruit might be painted realistically or imaginatively; some bore cheery, whimsical faces. My grandmother often said, "Come into my kitchen so my fruit can see you!"

Women would collect and arrange pieces artfully on a kitchen wall, well into the '60s. Chalkware is fragile, though, so these fun bits of kitchen kitsch are getting hard to find today.

Kitchen grease often accumulated in the crevices, attracting dust. Woe to those conscientious homemakers who tried to soak the grease off in dishwater, ruining both paint and plaster. Gentle spot cleaning with a dry, soft cloth, no matter how gritty or discolored the piece, is the better method. (Don't try to retouch chipped spots; chalkware is so porous that the paint is likely to spread.)

You might still find pieces at rummage or estate sales, or online. Look for undamaged, unretouched, detailed pieces in bright colors.

And who knows? Today, everyone's trying to eat more fruit and veggies, so a nostalgic "fruit wall" might even serve as a gentle reminder when you snack!

‹ This large handsome piece is unmarked, but its size and excellent condition mean it could sell for more than other pieces. Watch those rummage sales!

This blushing little fruit still bears a 59-cent price tag, along with a 1947 copyright indicating it was made in Chicago.

FUN FACTS

By any other name
Chalkware looks like chalk, but it's not. "Plaster of Paris ware" would be a more accurate name, but just not as catchy.

Where to find it?
Check out rummage and estate sales, flea markets and antique malls, websites like *etsy.com* and *ebay.com*.

Going bananas
In the 1940s, fresh fruit was enjoyed only seasonally. The bananas we take for granted today were a huge novelty; Miss Chiquita Banana's 1944 radio jingle was designed to teach people how to ripen and store them. People went bananas for the jingle—at its peak, it was played 376 times a day on U.S. radio stations.

Choices abounded for grocery shoppers in the 1960s. Talk about variety: By the end of the decade, a typical supermarket offered consumers nearly 8,000 different products.

When Shopping Was *Super*

The supermarket boom reflected the country's burgeoning prosperity.

BY RACHAEL LISKA

Grocery shopping in the 1950s and '60s was anything but a mundane chore. Cruising the plentiful aisles of a supermarket was part social outing and part escape into a novel, gee-whiz world of new technology.

It wasn't unusual to see homemakers dress their best, from perfectly coiffed hair to nice dresses to high-heeled shoes. They perused aisles stacked with exciting new convenience foods such as frozen Eggo waffles and powdered Tang to TV dinners and SpaghettiOs that promised kitchen liberation. Grand openings of gleaming modern supermarkets were the talk of the town.

No doubt about it: The supermarket experience was special, a reflection of the optimism and prosperity that defined the era.

It wasn't always so. A clerk behind a counter used to pull items from shelves and measure out dry goods for customers. But businessman Clarence Saunders revolutionized the way we buy food when he opened his first Piggly Wiggly store in Memphis, Tennessee, in 1916. This "self-service" operation featured open aisles lined with shelves (hello, impulse buying!), shopping baskets and front-of-store checkout counters. America's take-charge, self-sufficient consumers never looked back.

Less than 15 years later, Michael Cullen made history by opening the nation's first supermarket: the King Kullen Grocery Co. store in Queens, New York. It boasted evening hours, a parking lot, low prices and a full line of

CLASSICSTOCK/ALAMY STOCK PHOTO

A MEATY TALE
In 1955, I got hired to wrap meat at Purity Market, the first self-serve meat market in Fort Bragg, California (that's me, second from left). The manager hired the first three girls who showed up for an interview—and I was the first one in line!
DOLORIS WILBUR
ORTING, WA

foods—meats, produce, baked goods—all under one roof.

The great supermarket expansion allowed chains to refine their images with more modern or themed exteriors. Does anyone remember Safeway's marquee red lettering, curved roofs and all-glass fronts? Or the motto plastered on every Publix storefront: "Where Shopping Is a Pleasure"? How about the colonial-style theme of the A&P's?

Grocers raised the bar again in the 1940s and '50s with modern interiors and in-store offerings, including wider aisles; lavish meat counters, where butchers cut and trimmed custom orders; lofty piles of fresh produce; and incentives like trading stamps. Freezers stocked with Swanson TV dinners and Mrs. Paul's fish sticks beckoned busy mothers.

Supermarkets continued to evolve in the '60s and '70s, introducing carpeting, showy colors, full-service delis and flower, toy and liquor departments. This period also marked the debut of deep discounting as consumers continued to demand ever-lower prices.

Nowadays, upscale stores like Whole Foods and supercenters like Walmart may reign supreme with shoppers. But the next time you head out of the house with your grocery list, remember how exciting food shopping used to be when it just meant a trip to the local supermarket.

DID YOU KNOW

DID YOU KNOW THAT IN 1870, MARGARET E. KNIGHT RECEIVED A PATENT FOR INVENTING A MACHINE THAT FOLDED AND GLUED PAPER TO FORM THE NOW-UBIQUITOUS FLAT-BOTTOMED PAPER GROCERY BAG? SHE WAS ONE OF THE FIRST WOMEN TO EARN A U.S. PATENT.

Cash registers had a separate slot where S&H green stamps came out. I can still see my mother sitting at her desk, licking the stamps and sticking them in books.

LISA MULLIGAN OVITT
VIA FACEBOOK

I always dressed up when we went to the grocery. For years, my husband and I would go together with our two sons. It was an evening out for us—with me in high heels. LOL!

JOYCE DAY • VENICE, FL

SHOPPING NIRVANA: CARTS, CONVEYORS AND UPC CODES

TO MAKE GROCERY SHOPPING evermore convenient and alluring—and to outsell the competition—operators constantly sought out innovations. Take the venerable grocery cart, for example. Sylvan Goldman, who owned a chain of Piggly Wiggly stores, invented it in 1936 when he added two wire baskets and wheels to a folding chair.

A couple of years earlier, Big Bear Store—the first self-service supermarket in the Midwest—rolled out another innovation when it became the first grocer to use cashier-operated motorized conveyor belts.

In 1940, George Jenkins, the founder of the Publix chain, opened Florida's first supermarket. His "dream" store wowed customers with such high-tech wonders as electric-eye doors, fluorescent lighting, piped-in music and air conditioning.

The first UPC scanner debuted in 1974 at a Marsh's supermarket in Troy, Ohio. The first item sold with a bar code? A pack of Wrigley's Juicy Fruit gum. And in 1981, Hill Refrigerator Works—established by C.V. Hill, a former New York grocer—gave customers a new way to look at food with the introduction of the first U.S.-manufactured curved-glass deli case.

STAMPS: PHOENIX CREATIVE/ALAMY STOCK PHOTO; CHECKOUT: CLASSICSTOCK/ALAMY STOCK PHOTO; TV DINNER: KITSCHSTOCK/ALAMY STOCK PHOTO

TV DINNERS TO THE RESCUE

WHEN MOM WAS THE WAITRESS

WHEN MY FATHER would work past dinnertime in the late '60s, my mother, my sister and I would play Miss. Our mom would be our waitress—"Miss"—for the night and let us each pick out a TV dinner. My favorite was turkey with stuffing and potatoes, and my sister always opted for the fried chicken and potatoes, care of Swanson.

We'd watch television while our dinners baked, and when they were ready, Miss would call us to the table. She'd hand us each a menu with our dinner written on it. We even got a drink with our supper, which we normally didn't get! We'd call Miss over to ask for things like drink refills and clean napkins. When we were through, Miss would bring us the bill.

We had so much fun playing with Mom on those nights!

BARBARA DELL • BETHPAGE, NY

A LOVE FOR MEAT LOAF

I REMEMBER MY FAVORITE childhood TV dinner: meat loaf in red sauce with a brownie on the side. I can still almost taste it.

In college, talking about favorite late-night snacks, all my friends said their favorite was a chicken TV dinner. I said I couldn't believe they picked chicken when they could have chosen anything! And that's when they said it: "The worst was the meat loaf." They glanced at me...the look on my face gave me away!

Some sweet soul said, "It must be much better than I remember. I'll have to try it again!"

KATHLEEN HEINZ • LEBANON, OR

If This Sink Could Talk

A modest kitchen was the source for many of this family's memories.

I recently inherited the house I grew up in, and the thought of owning the home my father built with his own hands was a little overwhelming. This house has been a living, breathing entity for so many years and now it's quiet, as if the building is anticipating its next role. I can't help but feel the same way.

Wandering through the familiar halls and rooms felt foreign. This place had never known that empty quietness when I lived here.

The last room I went to was the kitchen—it was the heart of our home. For decades, we made all our major family decisions around the kitchen table. From deciding which crops to plant to mourning a loved one, most of it happened in that room. Sticking out among the memories was the old, chipped, scratched, beat-up kitchen sink. There, in that sorry-looking cast-iron basin, were so many of our family's memories.

That sink was my first bathtub, and my brothers' as well. Even my own daughter was bathed there when we came to visit.

The aged chips and scratches pointed toward moments in family history. There was the time Mom dropped a heavy pan in the sink to get Dad's attention. Her tactic worked, but it left a large scar in the middle of the sink.

I can still remember when my brothers and I were arguing, and Mom put the three of us in different corners of the dining room to scold us. In the meantime, she caught a glimpse of something bright in the kitchen. Flames reached a foot high out of a frying pan on the stove. Mom ran to the kitchen, grabbed a potholder and threw the fiery skillet into the poor sink. The flames went out immediately, but there were battle scars to show for it—another serious chip and some new scratches.

I was a little hard on the sink as a kid, too. I once threw a handful of table knives into the sink because I was mad I had to clean the table rather than get to play outside. The knife handles created several new chips and Mom made me clean the table for one week for each new ding. I'm not sure how Mom knew which chips were new, but I'm sure it bought me six weeks of kitchen duty.

Mom wanted to replace this sink for so long, but Dad could never find the time or the resources to do it. The sink often had to wait because some piece of farm equipment needed to be fixed. I'm glad Dad won out.

I'm eager to live the new chapters of our family's history in this same kitchen. I may change my mind and replace this sink someday, but not now.

STEPHEN FRENCH • CONCORD, NC

SINK: ISTOCK.COM/JIMSCHEMEL

THE BEST START TO A DAY

Our family made a point of sitting down to breakfast before starting a busy day at school or work. From left are myself, Niel, Marianne, Lyle and Mom Florence. Seventeen at the time, I admit that I liked to pour chocolate milk on my cereal. I was too busy digging into my bowl to look at my dad snapping this photo in 1947.

DON KRUEGER • DELAFIELD, WI

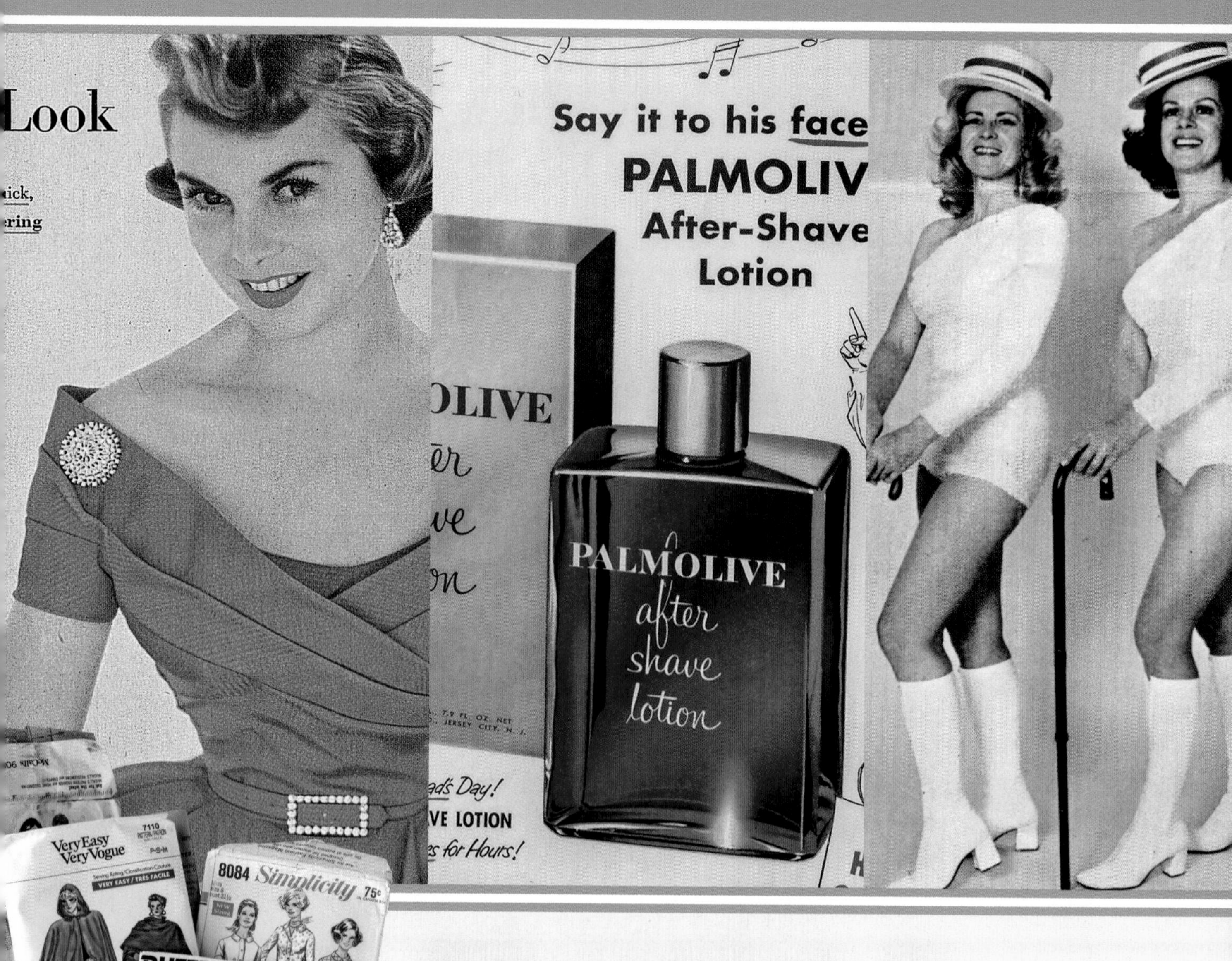

BEAUTY & FASHION FADS

CHAPTER 2

The products and techniques have changed through the years, but looking good has always been an endless pursuit. The clothes we wear reflect the times and our own fabulous personalities.

Ding Dong, Avon Calling

Learning the ropes brought out her inner sales diva.

After relocating to Hays, Kansas, in 1976, I began searching for a part-time job. I didn't want to go to an office every day and had heard about the benefits of becoming an Avon lady. I figured I could do that job from home, so I called the district manager.

I was assigned a certain territory and told to stay there. In those days, representatives were not allowed to sell to someone in another territory.

My manager told me that to be most effective I should visit everyone in my 100-house territory. So I did just that. She also told me that to net more sales, I should purchase demos or products I could show to customers, so I tried that, too. I bought every demo I could and began racking up sales.

During one two-week campaign, I bought a bath brush as a demo and sold eight of them. Another time I purchased a blush stick to demo and sold a ton of those. My then-husband commented that I could probably sell refrigerators to Eskimos. Within three months I became the top sales representative out of roughly 40 in my district.

By 1981, I had maintained my position as the district's top sales rep. About that time, my

AVON THROUGH THE YEARS

Browse the milestones achieved during Avon's first 132 years in operation.

1886
Bookseller David H. McConnell founds the California Perfume Co. Mrs. P.F.E. Albee becomes the first company sales rep.

1896
The company issues its first brochure.

1920
Sales top $1 million.

1939
The company is renamed Avon Products Inc.

1946
Avon goes public.

1954
Company launches the "Ding Dong, Avon Calling" campaign, one of the longest and most successful ad campaigns in history.

1955
The Avon Foundation begins with a $400 scholarship; in 2009 it is renamed the Avon Foundation for Women.

manager, who was planning to retire soon, approached me about becoming the district manager. It was unusual for a manager to be from her own local district, but because I'd worked alongside the reps, they accepted me as their new boss. I shared with them the secrets of my success and in turn helped them to be successful.

I was in charge of seven counties in western Kansas, and within my first year I won a trip to Hawaii. My division manager never informed me just how successful I was, but an announcement came at the yearly Avon recognition banquet that my district was No. 10 out of 3,000 in the entire nation. For that I won a trip to Monaco.

By 1983 I had relocated from western Kansas to Denver, Colorado, and contacted the same division manager about working for her again. Her comment to me was, "Tell me what district you want and I'll open it up for you."

I worked with her as a manager for another year but wanted to move up in the company. At that time, however, Avon was experiencing a reorganization, and no higher-level positions were available. I felt I had accomplished everything I had wanted to and left the company.

One benefit of my door-to-door sales calls was that I made many friends as customers. One woman I met about 35 years ago became my best friend. It was an incredibly rewarding time and I am very grateful for all of my Avon experiences.

PHYLLIS VALENS • DERBY, KS

COLLECTION (30558368); AVON LADY: COURTESY OF HAGLEY MUSEUM & LIBRARY; COMPACT: OLLI_MAY/SHUTTERSTOCK

BY THE NUMBERS

5
Single-note fragrances in the company's first product, the Little Dot Perfume Set

$400
Avon Foundation's first scholarship grant

6 MILLION
Avon representatives as of 2009

$1 BILLION
Contributions to women's causes from Avon and Avon Foundation for Women

143
Countries where Avon is sold

1961
The company introduces Skin-So-Soft, one of its most recognizable brands.

1971
Avon begins selling jewelry.

1978
Avon boasts 1 million reps worldwide.

1986
Avon introduces BioAdvance, the first skin care product to use stabilized retinol, a vitamin A derivative.

1989
Avon becomes the first major cosmetics company to end animal testing.

1999
Andrea Jung is named Avon's first female CEO.

2008
Company sales soar to $10 billion.

2016
Avon Products Inc. and New Avon LLC became separate companies.

2017
Actress Eva Mendes becomes the face of Avon's new launch, Eve Duet, a double-sided spray perfume.

FRESH (FAMOUS) FACES

Celebrities have been used to sell products for about as long as there have been products to sell. And in the 1940s and '50s, magazine ads glowed with Hollywood glamour.

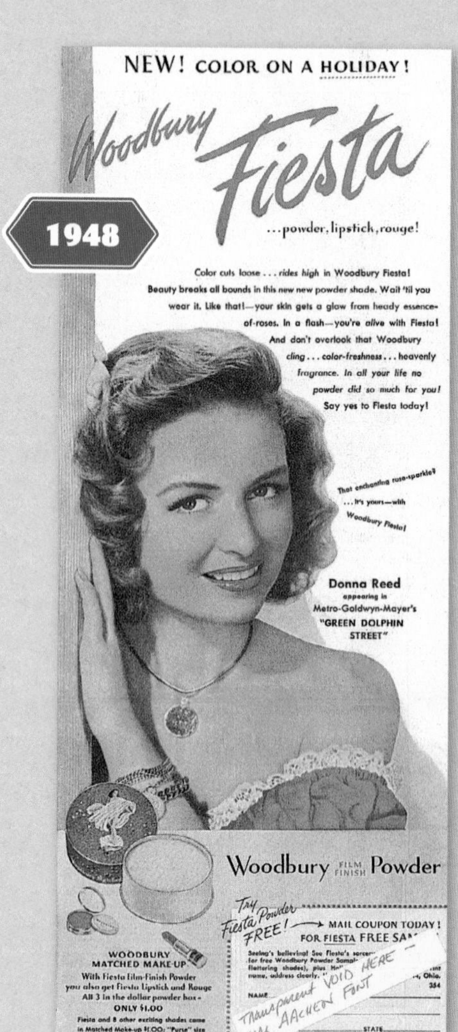

At left, Donna Reed promotes Woodbury Fiesta cosmetics and her new film, *Green Dolphin Street*. Above, Janet Leigh poses beautifully for Max Factor in Pan-Cake Make-Up. Her new film, *Scaramouche*, is mentioned.

Maureen O'Hara touts Max Factor's new lipstick and includes a callout to her new film *Sinbad the Sailor*. At far right, Ann Miller appears in an ad for Max Factor promoting her new movie, *Carolina Blues*.

1947

1944

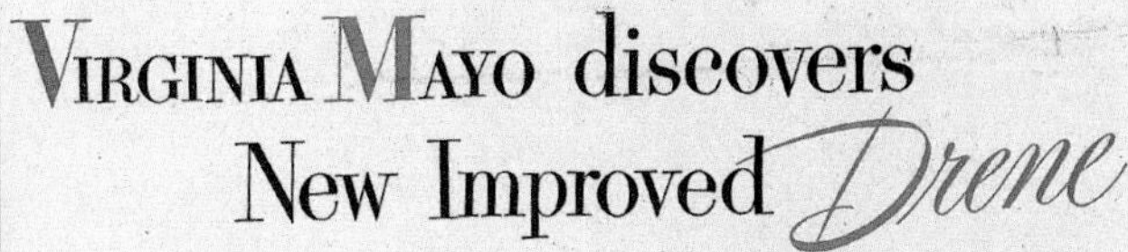

1947

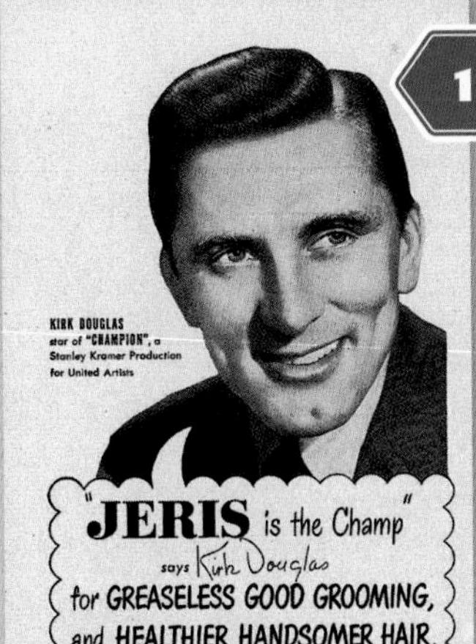

1950

At far left, Virginia Mayo shows off her hair for a Drene shampoo ad that also mentions her new film, *The Secret Life of Walter Mitty*. Near left, a young Kirk Douglas smiles for Jeris and as the star of *Champion*.

BYE-BYE, BEARDY

Americans paid increasing attention to personal hygiene in postwar years, and because cologne was widely regarded as effeminate, aftershave emerged as a more macho alternative for men.

1947

Today, McKesson focuses on health care supplies—but in decades past, it made toiletries under its Tawn division. "Man Alive" indeed—who could resist this guy's gleeful grin?

Before Old Spice became a trusty gift standby to "add spice to Dad's life," it was a fragrance for women called Early American Old Spice, which debuted in 1937.

It was typically girlfriends and wives who introduced aftershave into men's lives, but in honor of Father's Day, Palmolive marketed its scented lotion in this ad with two children.

GRANDFATHER'S SHAVING MUG

IN MY CURIO CABINET, I have a beautiful Limoges porcelain mug with the initials TJP. It's not a tea or coffee cup, but a shaving mug that belonged to my grandfather, Thomas Joseph Potts.

Thomas was a clerk for the Pennsylvania Railroad. He and Margaret, my grandmother, had six children, the eldest being my father, Thomas Jr. They lived in a house provided by the railroad on Pittsburgh's South Side. My father and his siblings had a happy childhood, with everything they needed.

That all changed when my grandfather died of a brain aneurysm in 1935. My grandmother was left to feed and clothe six kids on her own. Often she would set the dinner table as though they were going to have a nice meal, but then could serve only bread and coffee to her children.

On the day her husband died, my grandmother took my dad aside and told him to run as fast as he could to the barbershop to retrieve the elder Thomas' shaving mug.

That mug sat on my father's chifforobe until he died, when my mother gave it to me.

I look at it and see the determination and love of a woman who wanted to make sure her son had something to remember his father by and to pass on to his own children.

LUANN PORTLER • ALIQUIPPA, PA

GO BIG OR GO HOME

Bouffants and beehives did for hair in the 1960s and early '70s what miniskirts did for legs—styles just kept getting higher and higher.

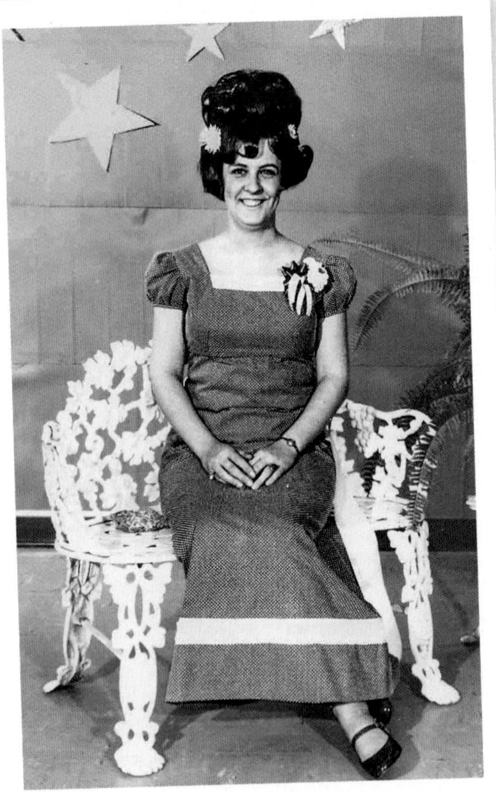

MORE SPRAY?
When I was in high school in Minnesota in the 1960s, you just weren't a part of the in crowd if your hair didn't match the width of your shoulders. I remember spraying my bouffant with Aqua Net until I could push on one side and the whole head of hair would move.
EVELYN KARPPINEN
MOORHEAD, MN

TRESSED TO IMPRESS
When I was 15 years old, I accessorized my beehive with fresh daisies. The occasion? An annual Valentine's Day banquet in the early 1960s at my church, in the Memphis, Tennessee, area. My mom, Frances South, made the gown of red dotted swiss. I remember feeling so special that night, like a princess.
BARBARA BIERBRODT
SOUTHAVEN, MS

COOL CAT
Hello, super 'do! For a wedding, it took my hairstylist quite a while and a lot of pins to updo all of my thick, long hair. I thought I was quite the cat's meow.
DEBBIE BRYANT
ROCKY RIVER, OH

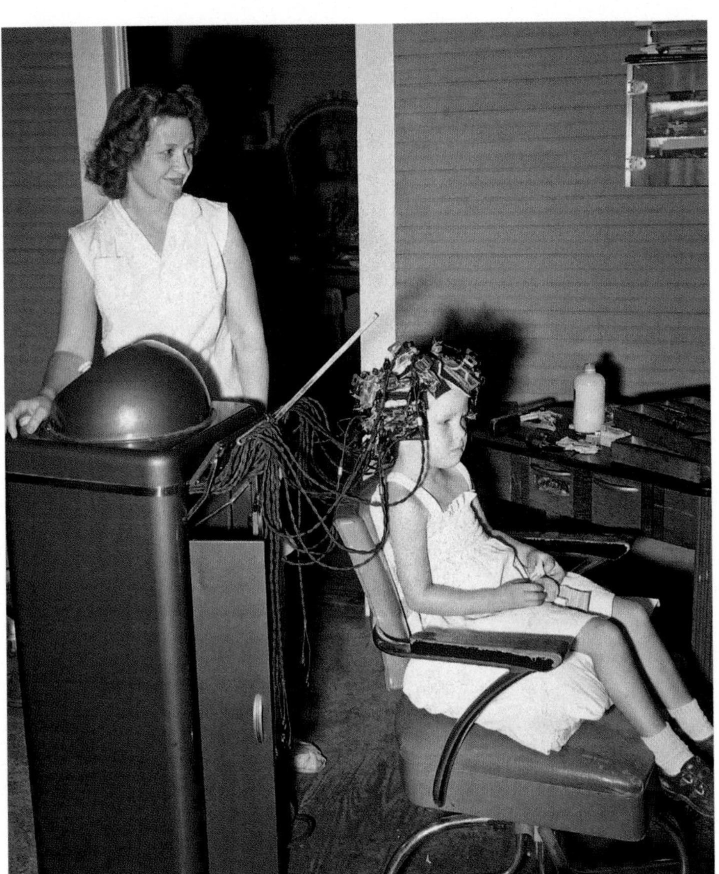

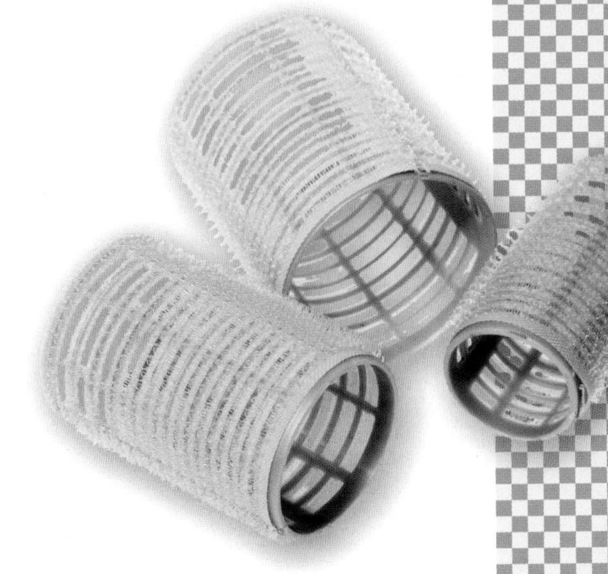

CURLY CUTIES

A friend of our mother's gave my sister Cheryl and me back-to-school perms in 1952 or '53; that's Cheryl in the chair with the odd-looking machine. I'm on the left in the smaller photo (below), showing off our finished results.

CAROL THOMPSON • GLENDALE, AZ

FRYING UP A HAIRDO

ONE FINE DAY IN LATE 1929, a lady walked into May's Beauty Shop, an establishment my mother operated in Monahans, Texas. The lady was in kind of a hurry, so Mother and her niece Geneva worked together to put her hair up for a permanent.

At the time, permanents were given with an electric machine. Each hair curl was covered with a metal sleeve connected to a wire from a contraption that supplied heat to the curl.

After going through the procedure, they had started taking down the curls when Mother unrolled a curl and saw the hair come off in the roller! At the same time, Geneva repeated the same catastrophe. Without making a sound, they looked up at each other in horror, not daring to let the lady know anything was wrong.

Mother said her knees went limp and her stomach turned over. Still, knowing them, I'm sure they had a hard time not giggling, regardless of how scared they were. It was a blessing the missing curls were in the back, and the customer wasn't facing a mirror.

They never saw that poor lady again, but Mom often wondered what she must have thought when she tried to comb her hair later—or how another beautician must have really cussed out the two of them!

WANIETA VESS INESS
LAS VEGAS, NV

CURLERS: KITTIBOWORNPHATNON/SHUTTERSTOCK

LUXURIOUS LOCKS

These promotions portray the humble beginnings of some favorite hair care products.

1933

Hairnets: They weren't always a lunch-lady mainstay. Lorraine sold a double-mesh line "for the woman who motors, rides, [or] plays golf."

In many Halo shampoo ads, glossy-haired "Halo girls" enjoyed an admiring male gaze.

JAMES DARREN co-starring in "THE GENE KRUPA STORY" a Columbia Pictures release

"You can always tell a Halo girl…you can tell by the shine of her hair"

1960

Discover the hidden beauty of your hair—with golden Halo Shampoo

Revive the satiny sparkle of your hair with today's liquid gold Halo

So rich even layers of dulling hair spray disappear with the first sudsing! You'll find today's Halo instantly bursts into lush, lively lather. Refreshes the beauty of your hair so completely, you'll never go back to heavy, slow-penetrating shampoos. Yet, rich as it is, liquid gold colored Halo rinses away quickly, thoroughly . . . revives the satiny sparkle of your hair and *leaves it blissfully manageable.*

WOMAN'S DAY FEBRUARY, 1960 15

1961

Roux's Fanci-Full Rinse became America's top temporary hair color during the '60s. To play her role in the 1997 film *As Good as It Gets* while still shooting her sitcom *Mad About You*, Helen Hunt used Roux's temporary rinse to alternate between brown and blond hair every other day!

SPRAYED, RATTED AND ROLLED

Some hairstyles really take on a life of their own, adding both poise and personality to the one donning the 'do.

STYLE FROM HEAD TO TOE

My dad actually talked me into getting my hair cut this way, and I loved it! This is my ninth-grade graduation picture. Don't you also just love the paisley Nehru jacket I was wearing?

MARCIA DEBOER
VIA EMAIL

STAYING POWER

Our hairstyles in 1965 required a lot of back-combing and hairspray. A 'do would last a week if we wore a net on our hair at night.

ANN JENSEN • BYRON, MN

THE FLIP

This hairdo was very popular in Camanche, Iowa, in 1964, when I was 15. If your flip rolled completely over, we called it a weenie roll. The little clip-on bows were an added touch. I've always liked this picture. Hard to believe it was more than 50 years ago.

CINDY LYKAM • LEWISVILLE, NC

DANCE 'DO

My bob was straight. In this photo, I was a school secretary dressed to chaperone the prom!

CAROL JACOBS NORWOOD
MYERSTOWN, PA

’50s Fashionable

Navy wife sewed up first prize—and international fame—in a McCall’s fashion contest.

When I started sewing at age 14, I never imagined it would lead to a trip to Paris and international media attention. But that’s exactly what happened in 1952. It all started with the purchase of a 25-cent McCall’s pattern. Talk about a great investment!

Contestants in the Easter Parade Fashion Contest had to use a McCall’s pattern as a starting point, but could customize and accessorize it. I chose pattern No. 8724 and used navy-blue gabardine to make a coat-and-dress ensemble that could be worn eight different ways by changing accessories.

I added a big white collar and cuffs, a cape and another set of cuffs in blue-and-white checked taffeta, a taffeta bow, a taffeta dress to wear under the coat, a yellow fleece bolero and a white corduroy jacket, all removable. I even whipped up a white hat from the fabric left over from the collar and cuffs. Total cost? About $13.50!

Out of more than 15,000 entries, mine was judged the most fashionable ensemble made by a home sewer. The prize was two weeks in Paris for two, all expenses paid. I went with my husband, Bob, a career naval officer who has since passed away. We even took an extra two weeks to explore other European cities.

When I got the telegram telling me I’d won, I couldn’t have been more thrilled. The first thing I did was call my mother. I’ll never forget her quip: “Well, now you’ll never have to scrub floors!”

Jeanne Herrick models her first-place creation in one of the photos sent to McCall’s.

The Herricks happily take off on their once-in-a-lifetime trip to France, Germany, Italy and much of Western Europe, having added their own time to the McCall’s trip.

Three-year-old son Bobby, seen with Jeanne and Bob at their home in Arlington, Virginia, knows he'll be staying with his grandmother in Sayre, Pennsylvania, as his parents see the sights in Europe.

Showing that her coat dress could be worn eight ways, Jeanne impressed the judges.

Almost from the moment we stepped off the plane in Paris, photographers from all over the world followed us around—even up the Eiffel Tower.

In addition to touring timeless Paris landmarks, we met and enjoyed a Champagne toast with Paul Coirre, head of the Paris city council. He presented me with a large scroll and a beautiful replica brooch of one designed for Queen Elizabeth when she was still a princess.

I also met with famous designers like Jacques Heim, who showed me how he draped models with certain fabrics to create interesting designs. I visited the workroom at Jacques Fath's design house, where the midinettes (seamstresses) and I compared techniques. I also got to see new collections at such glamorous houses as Christian Dior, Elsa Schiaparelli and Jeanne-Marie Lanvin.

Later, while in Rome, we were sitting at a sidewalk cafe and saw a newspaper with a story about me. I think the reason our trip got so much attention was that my dress showed you didn't have to be a famous Paris designer to turn out eye-catching fashions.

My own clothes, made from McCall's patterns, drew many compliments. But I left my winning ensemble home, because I was tired of modeling it by then!

I started sewing because of my mother, who made all our clothes during the Depression and liked us to be well dressed. I don't remember paying a whole lot of attention to how she sewed, but I must have absorbed quite a bit.

I remember my first sewing effort at age 14: a flowered voile dress with velvet ribbon run through white eyelets. I adored that dress. My sister, Jane, must've figured that others would, too. Coincidentally, one day I saw a woman wearing my exact masterpiece as she walked down the street!

My mischievous sister admitted she'd sold it to the lady—I think it was for 50 cents—and Mom bought

At the height of my sewing days, I made about one garment a week. I had three closets full.

The basic dress, made from the McCall's pattern on the opposite page, got a number of creative tweaks from Jeanne.

it back, then gave Jane a thou-shalt-not-steal lecture. I laughed when I read an old diary from that time; I wrote that a set of cotton shorts I made for myself was well worth the cost, which was 85 cents!

I got serious about sewing after Robert and I got married. When he wasn't flying blimps, he was studying for college courses at home, so he was busy all the time. I liked to "accomplish something," as I used to say. So instead of playing bridge, I sewed up a storm.

I remember Mom telling me that our son, Bobby, would never learn how to talk because all I did was sew while he sat in a playpen. I laughed and told her that it wasn't true—I always took him with me to buy more fabric! He proved her wrong, too: He went on to speak not just English but fluent Russian.

I never sewed for others, only myself. I loved to combine features from various different patterns to fashion something completely original.

While other kids my age were interested in things like roller-skating, I was intrigued by beautiful clothes. When I was growing up, women wouldn't go to the grocery store without wearing their hats and gloves. That's the way a proper person dressed.

At the height of my sewing days, I made about one garment a week. I had three closets full of clothes; there was always another outfit I wanted to make. I never minded when fashions changed, since I could always make whatever I wanted.

I never had a formal sewing lesson and I never learned to read a pattern in detail. I just put the pattern on the material and started chopping.

I no longer own the navy-blue outfit that earned me that special once-in-a-lifetime trip. I gave the ensemble to a maid who worked at the U.S. Embassy in Moscow, where we lived while Robert was a naval attache.

But I still have countless memories of outfits I designed and sewed with my own hands over the years, clothes that looked smart and drew admiring glances—and that for a little while made me the most famous home sewer in America.

JEANNE HERRICK
DUNN LORING, VA

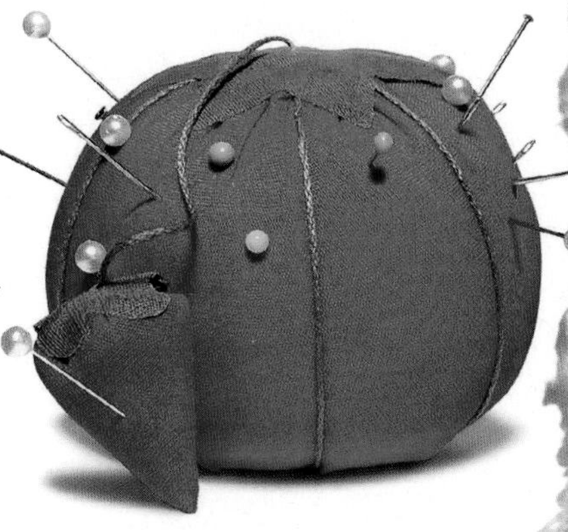

A PATTERN FOR SUCCESS

When it comes to fashion, Jeanne Herrick has one rule above all: Don't follow the crowd.

"I don't like to be told what to wear and what not to wear. I like little touches that nobody else thinks of." As for the advice to get rid of clothes not worn for a year or so, Jeanne doesn't buy it: "Maybe that's why I still have 3,000 things to wear, plus accessories!"

Fashion Do's

- **Cinch belts.** "I must have more than 100 of them," Jeanne says. "They take about 2 to 4 inches off your waist."
- **White or black pants** with blouses or loose-fitting jackets of virtually any color—and don't forget an eye-catching belt. "You can make it as simple or as fancy as you want to."
- **Costume jewelry.** "It offers you so much variety at a reasonable cost."

Fashion Don'ts

- **Designer-label clothes.** "Just a pathetic way for people to draw attention to their bank accounts."
- **Short skirts.** "They're just not right for public dressing."
- **Above-the-knee dresses.** "They're really tunics. It looks like you left off half the outfit."
- **3/4-length sleeves.** "It looks like the factory ran out of fabric!"

VINTAGE ADS

DO-IT-YOURSELF COUTURE

The right tools make it look easy.

Singer had retooled for the war effort, but its network of Sewing Centers sustained its domestic market mainly through rentals and sales of used machines. This ad encourages sewers to update old styles with fancy buttons and add-ons like lace collars.

1944

The original Butterick pattern 6015, otherwise known as the walk-away dress, became a 1950s hit. The dress was so easy to make, you could start it after breakfast and walk away wearing it by lunchtime.

1954

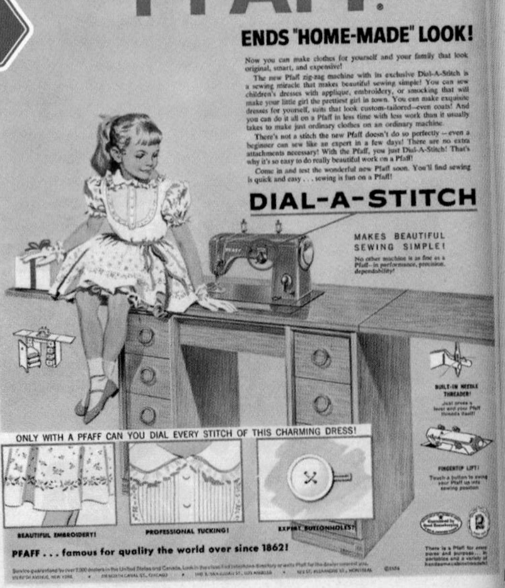

German maker Pfaff entered the consumer sewing market later than rival Singer, but it quickly gained a reputation for advanced design. This zigzag model boasted automated features for adding expert-level trim such as embroidery and tuck pleats.

IN STITCHES

The Big 4 pattern companies made fashionable clothing accessible to women who sewed. For many, the hardest part was finding the right fabric.

DURING THE 20TH CENTURY, most young women learned to sew in school classrooms using patterns available from the Big 4: Butterick, McCall's, Vogue and Simplicity.

Today's home sewers visit online communities where they get instruction, feedback and video lessons.

1863

Butterick began in 1863 when Massachusetts tailor Ebenezer Butterick created graded patterns for children of different sizes in response to his wife's suggestion. He also was the first to use tissue paper for patterns.

1870

The **McCall Pattern Co.** launched seven years after Butterick in 1870. In 2001 the company acquired both Butterick and Vogue, only to be purchased 15 years later by CSS Industries.

SEW YOUR OWN? › Vintage patterns range from $1 to $9 (this one originally sold for 35 cents!), but it takes skill to tailor them so the results will "fit like a glove."

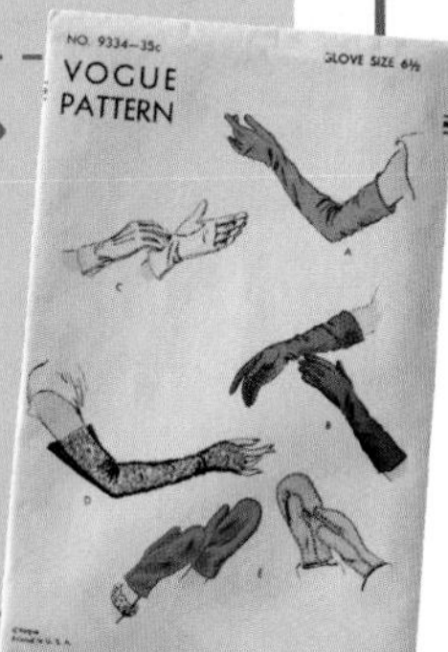

1905

Vogue Pattern Co. started in 1905 when Rosa Payne approached *Vogue* magazine about getting her pattern reproduced. The editor agreed, and soon the magazine was running clip-and-mail coupons; readers sent in 50 cents for a hand-cut pattern.

1927

Simplicity Pattern Co. was initiated in 1927 to capitalize on home sewers' desire to make fashion-forward clothing during the Depression. The company, later renamed Simplicity Creative Group, was purchased in 2017 by CSS Industries.

WALK-AWAY DRESS ILLUSTRATION: CSS INDUSTRIES

Maureen O'Hara, an Irish-American film actress, is seen here in 1947 in a fabulous hat. Bird feathers, bird wings and actual birds themselves were sometimes used to decorate hats, which is frowned upon today, and illegal in most instances.

HATS OFF TO SPRING

From veiled caps to pillbox hats, midcentury toppers turned heads.

Mention spring hats and most people think of Easter or the Kentucky Derby. But years ago, playful or dramatic chapeaus commonly topped off a woman's spring outfit. In earlier centuries, women donned bonnets and other head coverings for modesty. By the 1900s, however, hats were fashion statements. A graceful, broad-brimmed picture hat or fancy jeweled turban could make a lady the envy of a room.

Hats evolved to accommodate the trends and hairstyles of the time. During World War II, headwear took an array of shapes, from Rosie the Riveter-inspired head scarves and military berets to extravagant halo hats. Hats downsized in the 1950s, when many women chose clip-on veils called fascinators or close-fitting caps. And in the '60s, when beehive hairdos set the fashion world abuzz, flowerpot tops returned to fashion, along with Jackie Kennedy's signature pillbox hat. After all, it was hard to fit an understated cloche over those mounds of hair.

Save for sun hats and winter wear, most women hung up their hats by the '70s. Gone were the flowery fashion pieces that welcomed spring decades ago. But these days there's good news for hat lovers: They're making a comeback!

BRIMMING WITH STYLE

After my friend Jennie got engaged in May 1948, we celebrated with a luncheon at the Sahara Club in Bluefield, West Virginia. We dressed up in our best hats—the bigger the better! I'm fifth from the right in a black-brimmed hat.

ROXIE HARRIS BAILEY • BLUEFIELD, WV

MAUREEN O'HARA: PICTORIAL PRESS LTD/ALAMY STOCK PHOTO

ONE FOR EVERY OCCASION

In years past, a gentleman wasn't dressed to leave the house until he donned a hat. Men tipped their hats to ladies and made sure to take them off when indoors.

TO EACH HIS OWN

My grandpa, Oliver Glen Poland, is the young man on the right wearing the felt "sock" hat. This picture was taken in 1917, and his hat was one of the many popular styles back then. Grandpa is posing with his good friends at the time. Three men, three different preferences for hats!

JUDA WOODS-HAMLIN
VINCENNES, IN

WHITIE WORE IT WELL

The photo above is of Whitie Bevins, a friend I knew in the '70s. He gave me this lovely picture of him in his fedora, which I have kept all these years.

CAROL GALLO McDANIEL • MARANA, AZ

MAN OF MANY HATS

At special times throughout his life, my husband, Mike, sported hats. He wore an off-to-school hat as a boy and a National Guard side cap as a man. Here, posing with his parents in 1947, he perches a fedora at a jaunty tilt. Later in life, he wore a cowboy hat while shoveling snow. But I think his best hat of all was that of a wonderful dad to three daughters and five sons.

PEGGIE KAMM BERGANTINO • NORTHFORD, CT

LOOKING SHARP

The hallmark of midcentury men's fashion was an impeccable profile to match the image of the square-jawed, confident male.

Interwoven's ads early in the 20th century showed handsome men in varying stages of undress, clipping hosiery to their sock garters—all very suggestive. By 1947, the company took the more conservative tack of dispensing with the models and opting for disembodied socks floating about innocently, like leaves.

Here's a rare signed ad from commercial illustrator Tom Hall, who handled the print advertising account for Chicago suit-maker Hart Schaffner & Marx for almost 20 years. His men's apparel ads often featured, as this one, an urbane man going about his work while a pretty woman (or two) admired him from afar. The small print indicates the man wears the "Pan American," a suit style Hart Schaffner & Marx designed using South American wools.

1947

THEY'RE BACK!

All of those famous Arrow Collar Styles! Here are 7!

Once again, you can select the *one* particular Arrow Collar style you like best! Once again . . .

You can select from *countless* smart patterns in oxford or broadcloth, with soft or fused collars, and your choice of French or regular cuffs!

ALL Arrow Shirts (look who's reminding who!) are "Mitoga" shaped-to-*your*-shape, and bear the Sanforized label meaning: "no fabric shrinkage over 1%!"

KENT

The fused collar featuring very short, widespread points.

ARDSLEY

Arrow's famous fused collar with short points, fairly widespread.

SUSSEX

The soft collar featuring very widespread points.

FENWAY

The new, slightly widerspread, button-down soft collar.

BRUCE

The low neck band, long pointed soft collar.

ARNO

The fused collar in widespread, regular length points.

BELMONT

The regular shape fused collar, which looks well on almost every man. Cluett, Peabody & Co., Inc.

Look for the ARROW TRADEMARK *ARROW SHIRTS* \$3.25 . \$3.95 . \$4.75

This 1940s array of male pulchritude is a throwback to the Arrow Collar Man, devised in the 1910s and '20s by artist J.C. Leyendecker (who also did the racy sock ads for Interwoven). The sexy Arrow Man got as much fan mail as film stars.

SWIMSUIT SENSATION

Through the decades, swimwear has definitely shifted from modest to shocking. Compared to today's string bikinis, those early suits look conservative—but at the time they made a splash!

SUMMERTIME, AND THE LIVIN' IS EASY

The teenage bathing beauty here is my mother, Martha "Marty" Villwock. The photo was snapped in the early '40s, in Long Beach, California.

MARK VILLWOCK CORREY • NORTH TUSTIN, CA

FUN IN THE SUN

That's my grandmother on the right, striking a pose in the 1930s. Grandma had a hard life, and it's nice to see that in spite of everything, she had good friends and happy times.

RUTH CAMPBELL • GLENDALE, CA

WHERE ARE FRANKIE AND ANNETTE?

I'm posing in a one-piece pink suit, while my sorority sister Dorie showed off a cute orange two-piece. The year was 1963, and we were both students at Pierce College in Woodland Hills, California.

DARLENE (THOMPSON) VAN HEMELRYCK • PAGE, AZ

A GLIMPSE OF STOCKING? SOMETHING SHOCKING!

My great-great-grandmother Melissa (Moore) Harris (left) and her daughter, my great-great-aunt Georgie Beulah Harris, are sporting swim dresses at Oak Bluffs, Massachusetts. The photo was taken in the early 1900s. Is Great-Great-Aunt Georgie showing off some leg?

WENDY BUTLER JONES • POMONA PARK, FL

RISK TAKER

While sunbathing at Reichards Lake in West Sand Lake, New York, my aunt Hazel Kachadurian Baxter sported this patterned swimsuit. It was pretty daring of her to wear a two-piece when this was taken in the late 1930s or early '40s!

BEVERLY DUELL-MOORE • XENIA, OH

RIO BY THE SEA-OH

This is me at a Rio de Janeiro swimming pool. Check out the swimsuit!

PERLETTE ALVAREZ
RENO, NV

POLKA-DOT PRETTY

My mom, Maria Luz Sanchez, worked as a stewardess in the 1960s and early '70s. During a layover in Karachi, Pakistan, she and her friends went crabbing with some local fishermen, and she relaxed on the boat in this polka-dotted two-piece.

MARIA RAMONA HANNIGAN • SAN FRANCISCO, CA

TRENDSETTERS
High hemlines were in style at the salon where my friends and I (second from the right) worked as hairdressers in the early 1960s.
MARILYN JACOBSEN
ELMHURST, IL

THE MINISKIRT REBELLION

For young women in the '60s, short skirts symbolized freedom.

The first miniskirt appeared in *Vogue* magazine. Unlike the thigh-baring styles seen today, it brushed just above the knee. But for young women, it was liberating. Suddenly, their legs were free to dance.

Like the Fab Four, the miniskirt came from across the pond. London designer Mary Quant—often credited as the mother of the mini—began shortening hemlines in the late 1950s, when she opened her store in Chelsea. Inspired by the ballerinas she watched as a child, Quant wanted to create clothes that allowed women to move. Her young customers embraced the sleek style, requesting that she make her skirts even shorter. Although other designers were trimming hems, too, Quant's shop became the fashion center of the emerging mod scene.

Once the Chelsea-girl look caught on in London and models like Twiggy rose to superstardom, the miniskirt made its way to the U.S. In 1967, ABC aired a television special called *The Mini-Skirt Rebellion*, which introduced the skimpy style to all Americans. To their parents' dismay, teens embraced the trend. If only they'd known hot pants were on their way just three years later.

FUN FACTS

- Mary Quant named her skirt sensation after her favorite car, the Mini Cooper.
- Thanks to the mini, pantyhose hit the market in the 1960s, replacing restrictive undergarments like garters and girdles.
- American clothing companies were reluctant to adopt the mini—until they spotted trendsetter Jackie Kennedy wearing one.

SIZZLER SISTERS
In the '60s I attended a Catholic grammar school. We'd roll the waistbands on our pleated plaid skirts to make them shorter. By the time I got to junior high in the early '70s, my sister and I wore short "sizzler dresses"—with matching bikini panties for modesty.
BRENDA REAMY • SARASOTA, FL

Bold pants like these worn by none other than Sonny & Cher were an everyday style essential for teens in the early 1970s.

THE BELL-BOTTOM BOOM

Before flared pants were in style, Navy men sported them at sea.

BY LEAH WYNALEK

The wider the bell, the bigger the fashion statement. As many former flower children and disco dancers can attest, bell-bottom pants were the trend to try on in the late 1960s and early '70s.

Long before baby boomers donned bell-bottoms, American sailors wore them for more practical reasons. Beginning in the early 1800s, enlisted men dressed in belled trousers so they could roll the bottoms up over their knees while swabbing the decks. The fashion world didn't adopt flares until the next century, when European designers started selling them in the mid-1960s.

By decade's end, the hippie movement had embraced denim bell-bottoms, pairing them with floral print tops and tie-dyed T-shirts. But bell-bottoms entered the mainstream in the '70s, thanks in part really to Sonny & Cher. When the husband-and-wife duo began hosting their CBS variety show in 1971, they introduced the trend to a national audience.

Bell-bottoms became a must-have during the disco era, and clubbers dressed in flares of all fashions, including full leisure suits. When disco fever cooled down, so did the popularity of these wide-legged wonders. You'll still find flared jeans in stores today, but they don't measure up to true bell-bottoms.

SONNY & CHER: KEYSTONE PRESS/ALAMY STOCK PHOTO

TRUE BLUE

I was one of the first girls to wear denim bell-bottoms in seventh grade, and I thought I looked pretty "in." I kept on wearing them through high school and college in the 1970s and donned some extremely wide-legged pairs out to discos.

ARLENE ASCENZO
TORRINGTON, CT

COOL FOR SCHOOL

Check out my wide-legged pants in this picture from my 1974 high school yearbook—I'm leaning on a Mach 1 Mustang. I had satin shirts that I paired with them and platform shoes.

BRAD DOLAN
CHATTANOOGA, TN

GAGA FOR GO-GO BOOTS

Hip teens of the 1960s and '70s got their kicks from wearing long, tall, sexy boots. Were you one of them?

STILL A FAN ›
Boots were definitely the fashion statement when I was a student at Henry C. Conrad High School (Wilmington, Delaware). Here I am in white lace-up boots and a belted sizzler skirt. I wore go-go boots to the All Class Reunion held in April 2016. Am I gaga for go-go boots? You bet I am! I have about 15 pairs in my closet, and I always will.
CLAIRE CIARLO AUSTIN · FREDERICKSBURG, VA

‹ POST-WEDDING ATTIRE
My husband, Mark, and I were just moments away from a honeymoon when this picture was taken next to a 1970 Plymouth Road Runner—our muscle car. On Sept. 4 in Batavia, New York, I had changed from my wedding dress into a three-piece hot pants outfit along with calf-high go-go boots. My new husband said that a lot of the guys took extra-long looks at my legs in those shiny white boots. He was proud of the looks I got from other guys.
BONNIE ABRAMS · FORT PAYNE, AL

MISSING BANDMATE? ›
I loved this outfit. It made me feel good about myself after just having a baby. Imagine my big surprise when I wore this to a show put on by a local act called the Rising Generation... and the ladies in the band were wearing the same thing!
MAE WAGNER MARINELLO
REDLANDS, CA

CHIC CHRISTMAS ›

Here I am showing off my new go-go boots in front of the family Christmas tree. With stacked heels that increased this 16-year-old's height by nearly 3 inches, the shiny white boots were a perfect complement to the cool lavender crushed-velvet outfit I also had received as a gift that year.

PAMELA BRYAN
SHEPHERDSVILLE, KY

THREE OF A KIND

As married 20-somethings with children, my sisters Deanna and Maureen and I (left in photo) dressed up to celebrate Thanksgiving at Deanna's house. We all laughed when we showed up in hot pants. My go-go boots matched my outfit's piping and white blouse with oversized collar. Deanna paired red lace-up boots with red plaid hot pants and tunic detailing. Maureen, the youngest sister, opted to go boots-free.

ROSEMARY CAMPBELL · CAMARILLO, CA

DYNAMIC DUO ›

Matching straw boaters, diagonal necklines and knee-high go-go boots created a star-worthy look for The Singspirations: LaVada Marlowe and me, on the left. We both wore white boots with miniskirts during the 1960s and '70s. As I recall, our similar wardrobes were what drew us, a soprano and mezzo-soprano, together at a Los Angeles Master Chorale rehearsal and inspired us to start our own act.

PHYLLIS REED
SUN CITY, AZ

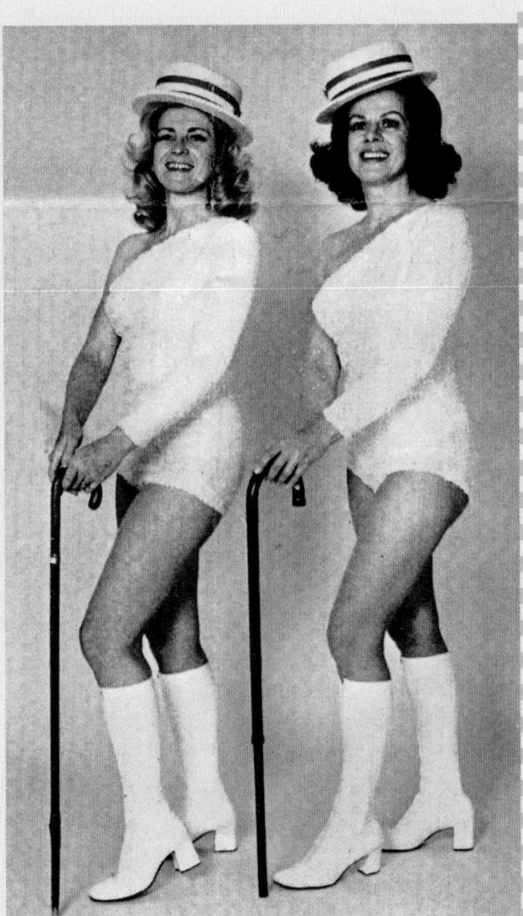

Be Dazzled

Peek into your jewelry box for potentially valuable finds.

BY JOE KENZ AND SANDY GARRISON

Let's clear up some easily confused terms regarding collectible jewelry. Estate jewelry is any piece previously owned and worn; it has nothing to do with age. Fine jewelry is made of high-quality precious metals such as gold, platinum or silver, while fashion or costume jewelry contains synthetic materials, gold plating or plastic. Vintage jewelry must be at least 20 years old; antique jewelry is more than 100 years old.

1 CAMEO

Cameos can be carved from a variety of shells and stones, featuring a range of images. The cameo pictured here is typical of the Victorian era, carved from a white shell with a coral background. Archaeological digs around that time increased interest in Roman mythology, and images of gods and goddesses became popular in cameos. Perhaps the agriculture goddess Demeter is represented here, given what appears to be wheat in the figure's hair, although the image could also simply represent a stylish lady of the time. This pin has a 14-karat gold and enamel border, and is estimated to be from around 1870.

BACK

FRONT

JEWELRY: SANDY GARRISON

② FUR CLIP

Wearing less expensive "costume" jewelry as a form of self-expression is a concept credited to Coco Chanel in the 1920s. The long, double-pointed clips on the back of this piece feature two sharp prongs attached to a spring, so they could pierce fur without damaging it. These features distinguish it from a dress clip, which has a wider, shorter clasp, and teeth meant for thinner dress fabric. This gold-plated clip was made in the 1940s by Coro, one of the manufacturers most coveted by collectors.

③ BROOCH

Enamel jewelry features a protective, decorative coating over metal—it's similar to the way dental enamel guards our teeth. Enamel in design can be traced all the way back to ancient Egypt and Persia. Enamel for use in jewelry gained newfound popularity during the art nouveau period as a way to incorporate rich color without using precious stones.

④ LOCKET

Lockets were popular from the 19th century up until World War II, although their origins can be traced to the 1500s. This one is art nouveau, a style popular in Europe and the U.S. from 1890 to 1910. The question-mark design on the front shows a common Victorian motif, and it's probable that this locket was a love token. It's gold-filled with clear rhinestones and in excellent condition.

⑤ BRACELETS

These art deco bracelets are made of rhodium, a metal more rare than gold or silver that is highly reflective and resistant to tarnish. The bracelets are made with the filigree process. Fine threads of metal are used to create intricate, lacy designs that are soldered onto the piece, a technique dating back to ancient Mesopotamia. Possibly German or French in origin, the bracelets pictured date to the 1920s or '30s and are decorated with enamel and rock crystals.

REUSE, REPURPOSE

- Create eye-catching napkin rings with a little bit of ribbon and costume jewelry.
- Make a plain winter hat shine by pinning on a brooch or sewing on other costume jewelry pieces.
- Fancy up a fridge door with a set of beautiful handmade jewelry magnets.
- Frame treasured heirloom brooches to display on the wall as artwork.
- For the holidays, add some shiny bling to a wreath, or try pinning brooches to gift bows.

Not His Most Model Moment

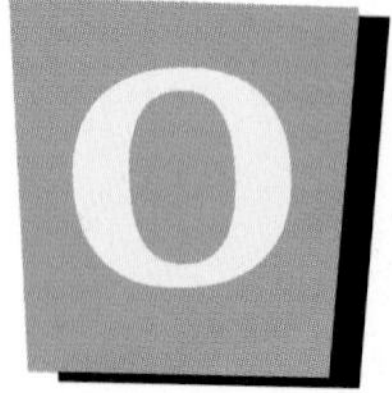

ne evening in 1951, I was in a show for Jacobs Junior Shop at the Hammonton High School auditorium in southern New Jersey.

The butterflies began to fill my tummy as soon as I entered the building, and they became absolutely unbearable when I was "on deck."

The fashion director had instructed me on the proper strut and the importance of keeping my eyes focused on the ribbon about 6 feet from the end of the runway. This functioned as a crude stop sign to prevent us from tumbling and requiring help from the local rescue squad.

I nervously kept asking those who preceded me, "Could you see anything with the bright lights shining in your face? Could you see the ribbon well enough?" Peeking from behind the giant curtain, I thought the narrow walkway truly resembled a gangplank.

Suddenly, I was next. The first 15 or 20 feet were just fine—I recall thinking about nothing but the ribbon. As I reached the object of my intense concentration and began my turnaround, my feet suddenly felt shackled, and I stumbled forward, landing on all fours. My fedora flew off and landed in the first row of the audience. There must have been a collective gasp as I ran off the runway toward the refuge of the backstage area, crying unabashedly.

I am told that the scene that night was so heartbreaking to everyone in attendance that my mom decided to purchase the entire wardrobe, which is probably hanging somewhere in the dark recesses of a closet as a pathetic reminder of the road not taken.

It is wonderful, though, how seemingly tragic events can become a source of great humor. How time does heal all wounds!

BILL DOMENICO • HAMMONTON, NJ

Bill modeling the latest fashions for Jacobs Junior Shop.

THOROUGHLY MODERN BETTY

The lady in this 1955 photograph is my wife, Betty. The picture was taken not only to show off my pretty wife and her dress but to spotlight our brand-new 19-inch Sears black-and-white TV. Betty is all dressed up to go dancing to some '40s and '50s music.

PAUL BRODE • HEMET, CA

TRAVELING BACK IN TIME

CHAPTER 3

What better way to get there than in style? Automakers and airlines alike are terrific at creating a sense of class and excitement when it comes to transportation. Let's go!

Road Candy

From 1949 to 1961, General Motors dazzled the world with its vision of our automotive future: Motorama.

When you're the biggest, richest company on the planet, you're entitled to a little shameless self-promotion now and then. That's how General Motors came to inaugurate a series of lavish auto shows designed to offer a tantalizing glimpse at the road ahead—for itself and America. With singing, dancing and live music (not to mention free admission), the shows were—in an era before TV advertising really took off—the ultimate corporate infomercial, drawing millions of wide-eyed car aficionados to places like the glitzy ballroom of New York's Waldorf-Astoria Hotel. The automobiles were the big draw, though. GM's charismatic styling chief Harley Earl coined the term "dream cars," and he made sure his gloriously futuristic rolling wonders lived up to that description every year. Take a look at a few favorites.

The jet-inspired Firebird XP-21 (later known as the Firebird I) headlined General Motors' 1954 Motorama, held in the ballroom of New York City's posh Waldorf-Astoria Hotel. The 1953 Motorama (the first show to use the Motorama name) saw the debut of a rakish little sports car called the Corvette (inset). Public reaction was so wildly positive that GM put the roadster into production later that year.

PREVIOUS SPREAD, CAR TAIL FIN: GRAPHICAARTIS/GETTY IMAGES; RIGHT: COURTESY OF GENERAL MOTORS, LLC (3)

WHO GOT IT STARTED

HARLEY EARL This charismatic Californian guided GM design from 1927 to 1958. He saw Motorama as a way to show off his futuristic concepts and tantalize the car-buying public.

MOTORAMA STARS

GM's dreamiest of dream cars.
What's your favorite rolling daydream?

1951

GM LE SABRE

WHAT IS IT? Indisputably the most famous and influential concept car of the 1950s, the road-worthy Le Sabre served as GM design chief Harley Earl's daily ride for two years after it returned from the Motorama circuit.
FUTURE FEATURE A water sensor that automatically raised the convertible top at the first sign of rain.

1951

BUICK XP-300

WHAT IS IT? As much an engineering exercise as a styling study, the XP-300 pushed the performance envelope.
FUTURE FEATURE With a lightweight aluminum body and a supercharged 335-hp V-8 engine, the XP-300 could hit 140 mph.

1953

CADILLAC LE MANS

WHAT IS IT? A low-slung two-seater created to commemorate Cadillac's run in the famous 24-hour race of the same name.
FUTURE FEATURE Cadillac's very first wraparound windshield.

1953

BUICK WILDCAT

WHAT IS IT? The first of three Motorama concept cars to use the Wildcat name (a production Wildcat arrived in 1963), this sleek roadster presaged the look of late-'50s Buicks.
FUTURE FEATURE "Roto-Static" stationary front wheel centers with integrated scoops that directed cool air to the brakes.

1954

BUICK WILDCAT II

WHAT IS IT? Another optimistic Corvette derivative, this one was meant to face off with MGs and Jaguars.
FUTURE FEATURE The Wildcat II made use of a 322-cubic-inch V-8—a year before the Corvette would move to eight cylinders.

1954

CADILLAC EL CAMINO

WHAT IS IT? Not to be confused with the Chevrolet car/pickup mashup that debuted in 1959, Cadillac's El Camino was a racy two-seat sport coupe with a 230-hp V-8 engine.
FUTURE FEATURE The tall tail fins, brushed stainless steel roof and quad headlamps offered a glimpse of future production models.

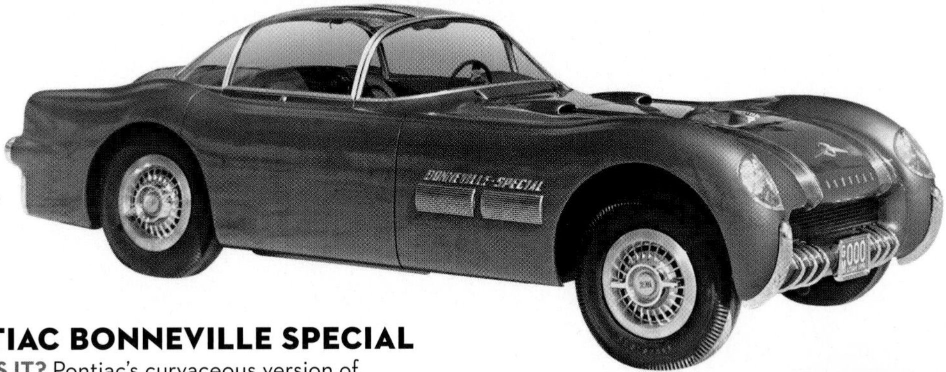

1954

PONTIAC BONNEVILLE SPECIAL

WHAT IS IT? Pontiac's curvaceous version of the Chevrolet Corvette, it never saw production.
FUTURE FEATURE A roof made of transparent Perspex acrylic, the same material used for the bubble canopies of military fighter planes.

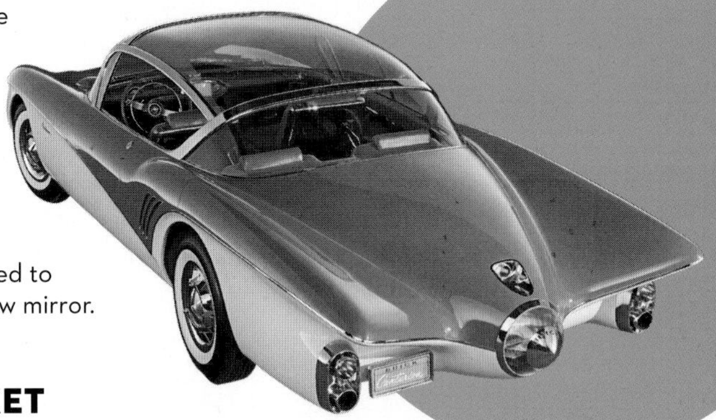

1956

BUICK CENTURION

WHAT IS IT? Despite its transparent top and fiberglass body, this coupe predicted Buick's style direction into the 1960s.
FUTURE FEATURE A rear-facing camera linked to a video screen in the dash, in lieu of a rear-view mirror.

1956

OLDSMOBILE GOLDEN ROCKET

WHAT IS IT? A lightweight, fiberglass-bodied sports coupe with a 275-hp Rocket V-8 engine.
FUTURE FEATURE When a driver or a passenger opened the door, the roof panel automatically raised and the seat lifted 3 inches and pivoted outward to ease entry or exit.

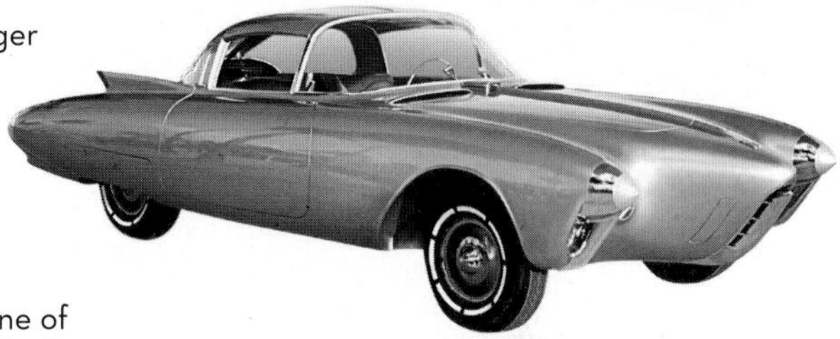

1959

CADILLAC CYCLONE

WHAT IS IT? This rocket-styled roadster was one of the most dramatic Motorama cars—and one of the last.
FUTURE FEATURE A crash-avoidance system that used radar sensors mounted in the car's nose cones.

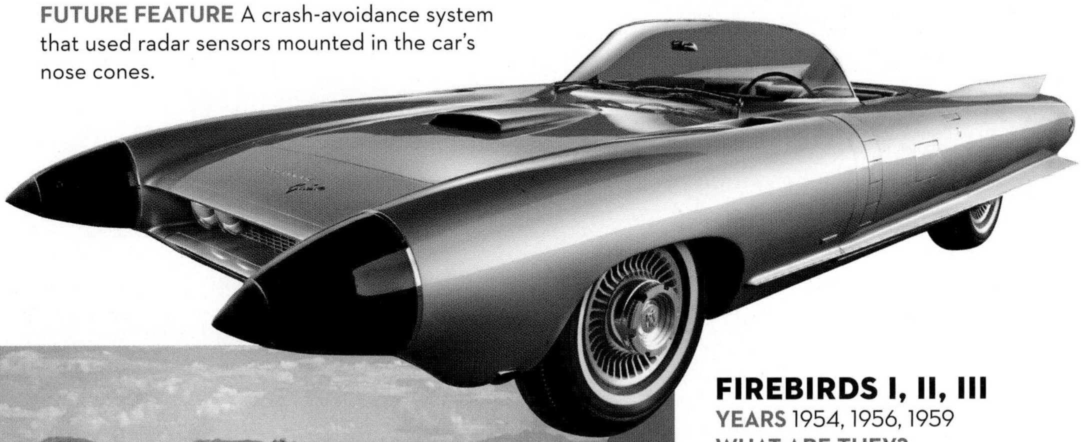

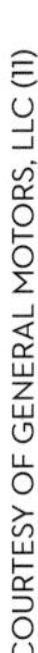

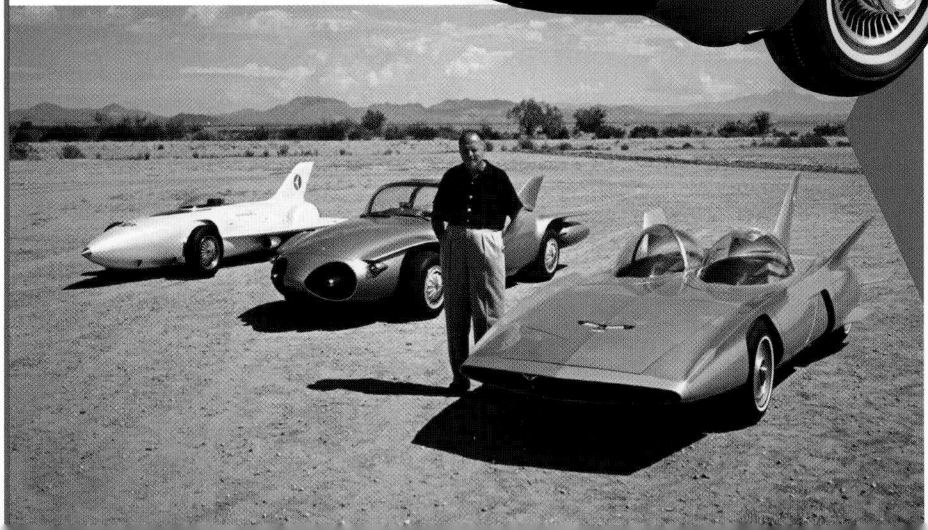

FIREBIRDS I, II, III

YEARS 1954, 1956, 1959
WHAT ARE THEY?
GM's wildest, most overtly jet-inspired visions of our motoring future, seating one, four and two, respectively.
FUTURE FEATURE The cars employed successively more efficient gas-turbine engines, similar to the engine that would power the Chrysler Turbine Car in the early 1960s.

COURTESY OF GENERAL MOTORS, LLC (11)

THREE DECADES LATER, A TREASURED CAR COMES HOME

He thought he'd never see that Camaro again. He was wrong.

AFTER I GRADUATED from junior college in 1968, I was back home in Pemberville and decided it was time to buy the Camaro I'd always wanted. I mulled over the possible choices for the '69 models, and picked the best one of all—the Super Sport (SS) package for the power and the Rally Sport (RS) trim for the luxury features like covered headlights, custom interior and rosewood steering wheel.

I was 19. I had enough for a down payment but needed my dad's help to get a bank loan. I wanted the 396-cubic-inch, 350-horsepower engine, but my father refused to co-sign my loan if I got that option. So I settled for 350 cubic inches and 300 hp.

I paid about $3,600 for the Camaro, which was delivered on March 18, 1969. I was so excited that I could barely work the four-speed shift to get it home, which was less than a mile from the dealer.

I drove my Camaro every day and drag-raced the country roads at night, mostly with friends who also had muscle cars. But in 1974, with my wife pregnant, we decided we needed a family car. I sold my beloved Camaro to a young man who lived a few miles away. He had it for a while until he sold it to someone else. I lost track of the car after that, assuming it was long gone or rusting away in a junkyard somewhere.

But in the summer of 1998, a car caught my eye at a small local show. It was a 1969 SS/RS Camaro with a black vinyl top and a metallic blue body. It had the same black custom interior, rosewood steering wheel, console and gauges as my old '69 SS/RS. It even had a Hurst T-handle on the gear shift lever, which I had installed on my car years ago. The woman who owned it lived about 15 miles from me. Just about the only difference between her car and my old one, I told her, was the color.

When she replied that her car used to be silver-gray, my heart started to pound hard. I told her whom I'd sold mine to and she smiled. His name was on an old vehicle registration for the Camaro that she kept in the glove box.

The Camaro had lived an interesting life with her: She'd replaced the engine and raced the car at area drag strips, winning several trophies.

I called her every spring for years asking if she'd sell it to me, but she always refused. Finally, in 2007, she was ready. The day I drove the Camaro home, I was as excited as I'd been on March 18, 1969.

These days, I drive the car about 600 miles a year, mostly to shows in the summer. I never drive it in the winter and I store it in a heated building. I won't let it get away from me again.

DENNIS LAYMAN • PEMBERVILLE, OH

After buying back his old Camaro, Dennis restored it to get it as close as possible to the car he bought in '69.

Jan loves to take Lola out for a cruise.

Her Name Is Lola, and She's a Showgirl

When I was 15 my next-door neighbor Gary got a 1971 Mustang Mach 1 as a graduation present. It was love at first sight for me. Growing up in the muscle car era, I had lots of favorites, from Chargers to Camaros. But the Mach 1 was in a whole different category. When I saw that sleek silver beauty with black racing stripes, I decided that someday I would own one.

In May 1976 I happened to pass a car lot and saw a bronze 1973 Mach 1. I couldn't turn around and get back to that lot fast enough. I talked my dad into co-signing the $3,000 loan, and a couple of days later that baby was mine. I named her Lola after the showgirl in Barry Manilow's "Copacabana (At the Copa)."

My boyfriend proposed to me in 1977, and I told him it was a package deal—me, my car and my springer spaniel, Brandy. He was fine with it. I'm fortunate that he was because he's a mechanical genius and keeps Lola in top shape.

When my kids were in junior high they were mortified if I used my "old car," as they called it, to take them to school. They'd beg to get out before we reached the school so they wouldn't be seen with it.

But once my son got to high school, my car suddenly became "pretty cool," and he was always asking to drive it. I'd just tell him, "Oh, you don't want to drive that old car." I never did let him drive it to school, but I did let him drive it to his wedding.

In 2005, we had Lola nicely repainted in her original color (saddle bronze) and she's as beautiful now as the day I got her 41 years ago.

These days she doesn't get driven too much anymore—mainly to cruise-ins, to car shows and on the occasional joy ride—but I still love the feeling I get every time I drive her.

My daughter summed it up best a few years ago when she said, "Wow, Mom, your generation had the cool music and cool cars!"

JAN HARTZOG • MISSION, TX

SHORT FOR POWER

Muscle car acronyms decoded

GS
Gran Sport

GT
Gran Turismo or Grand Touring

GTO
Gran Turismo Omologato

R/T
Road/Track

RS
Rally Sport

SS
Super Sport

Tony and Joan Przasnyski's restored 1955 Dodge truck joined them in their 2015 Christmas card.

A Full-Time Hobby

Staying busy in retirement involves a labor of love for one car enthusiast.

I'm retired, and my wife, Joan, and I spend the majority of our time at our 1980s-era log cabin kit home in Pennsylvania's Pocono Mountains. I was born with the car gene, so my retirement years seemed the right time to fix up a vintage truck. But what kind?

In 2010, I saw a neglected 1955 Dodge C-1 half-ton truck advertised on Craigslist. I contacted the seller to see if it would be a good fit for my retirement project. When I arrived at the seller's house, I discovered a neglected hot rod. The truck had maintained its original look, but it had been converted to a 1980s V-8 drivetrain long ago. With the truck's vintage style and modern power, it looked like the right candidate, but I went home to ponder my decision.

A few days later, the owner called and said that he was relocating and needed to find a good home for the truck. He slashed the asking price. The rest is history.

The truck turned out to be a bit rare, and this meant that many reproduction parts were unavailable. My search to replace damaged and rusted body panels sent me on road trips to various states to find better parts. My oldest son, Anthony Jr., helped me with the restoration. A car lover, he had remodeled a 1932 Ford Roadster to resemble a hot rod.

My hobby certainly did keep me busy—I finished the restoration in 2014. Now Joan and I drive the truck everywhere. We can hardly leave a gas station without a big crowd of admirers forming around it.

TONY PRZASNYSKI • COLLEGEVILLE, PA

GRAY TRUCK: ANTHONY PRZASNYSKI JR.

FURY IS REALLY A JOY

MOST PEOPLE DON'T forget the first car they ever owned. That's especially true for me, because I still own my first car, which I bought in 1966—a 1959 Plymouth Sport Fury.

I bought the car used for $800 in my senior year at Sunnyside High School in eastern Washington state. It took me three years to earn the money by doing part-time farm work for $1.25 an hour.

I drove it for three years, until the transmission gave out. After that, it sat and slowly deteriorated on my parents' farm until I hauled it to my current place in Michigan.

I've spent about 2,000 hours over seven years bringing the car back to its former glory. I was able to find all the original parts needed, including an overrun remnant of seat fabric. The restored beauty began its new life in a 2009 Memorial Day parade.

Getting behind the wheel on nice days certainly brings back wonderful memories. I love to drive it on summer evenings with my wife, Merrie Beth.

JOHN DEN BOER • SHELBYVILLE, MI

DID YOU KNOW

THE FURY DERIVES ITS NAME FROM NETHERWORLD GODDESSES OF VENGEANCE IN GREEK MYTHOLOGY.

The Fury was produced from 1959 to 1978, but this particular model was made in only 1959 and 1962 to '71. For 1959, the car was only available as a two-door hardtop or convertible.

SWEET RIDES

Wouldn't it be terrific to take a long Sunday drive in one of these vintage autos? Or better yet, own one? These folks were lucky enough to have spent some time behind the wheel of some super sharp-looking cars.

ROLLING BACK THE YEARS

I bought this 1966 Mustang convertible in honor of my dad, who died of cancer. In 1966, he got my mom a Mustang because he thought it would be a fun family car, and it was. I'm posing at a vintage Pure Oil gas station, which has significance to me because Dad worked periodically at a Pure station in addition to his 43 years at the Ford plant in Brook Park, Ohio.

JEFFREY LOUIS • HUDSON, OH

MISS INDEPENDENT

Mom bought this car on her own. She is the woman sitting behind the wheel. The other women are her sisters. Mom told me her dad was really angry when she got it. He said only hussies had cars! Mom got a job and moved out because her dad was so angry.

SAM BURCHFIELD
WICHITA, KS

CAN'T KEEP 'EM DOWN

In this picture, my darling wife, Margaret, and I are standing beside our 1965 Corvette roadster the day after our wedding in November 1971. We were preparing to leave the next day for Minneapolis on our honeymoon, and we were eager to hit the road and begin our lives together. About 70 miles north of Minneapolis, a valve rocker arm broke, leaving us stranded on the side of the highway. Fortunately, I had a toolkit on board, so I removed the rocker arm and walked 2 miles into a nearby town to buy a new one. I still have the broken rocker arm in my dresser drawer as a reminder of our adventures.

DON BARBINI • THUNDER BAY, ON

PURPLE PASSION

In 1953, when I was 20, I worked in an auto body shop in Zion, Illinois. I was customizing my 1947 Ford convertible when a paint salesman presented me with a can of the most beautiful purple paint I'd ever seen. The new color was a paint company experiment, the stuff was free, and I couldn't resist! My friend Peggy Taylor is standing by the Ford in the picture.

JOHN BEEBE • HIAWASSEE, GA

TWO-TONE FUN

On this sunny day in 1956 my wife, Barbara, and I enjoyed a tailgate picnic at the beach in Caseville, Michigan. It's hard to say which stands out more: that candy-striped Ford station wagon or Barbara's colorful capris.

WALTER MOHR • MILLINGTON, MI

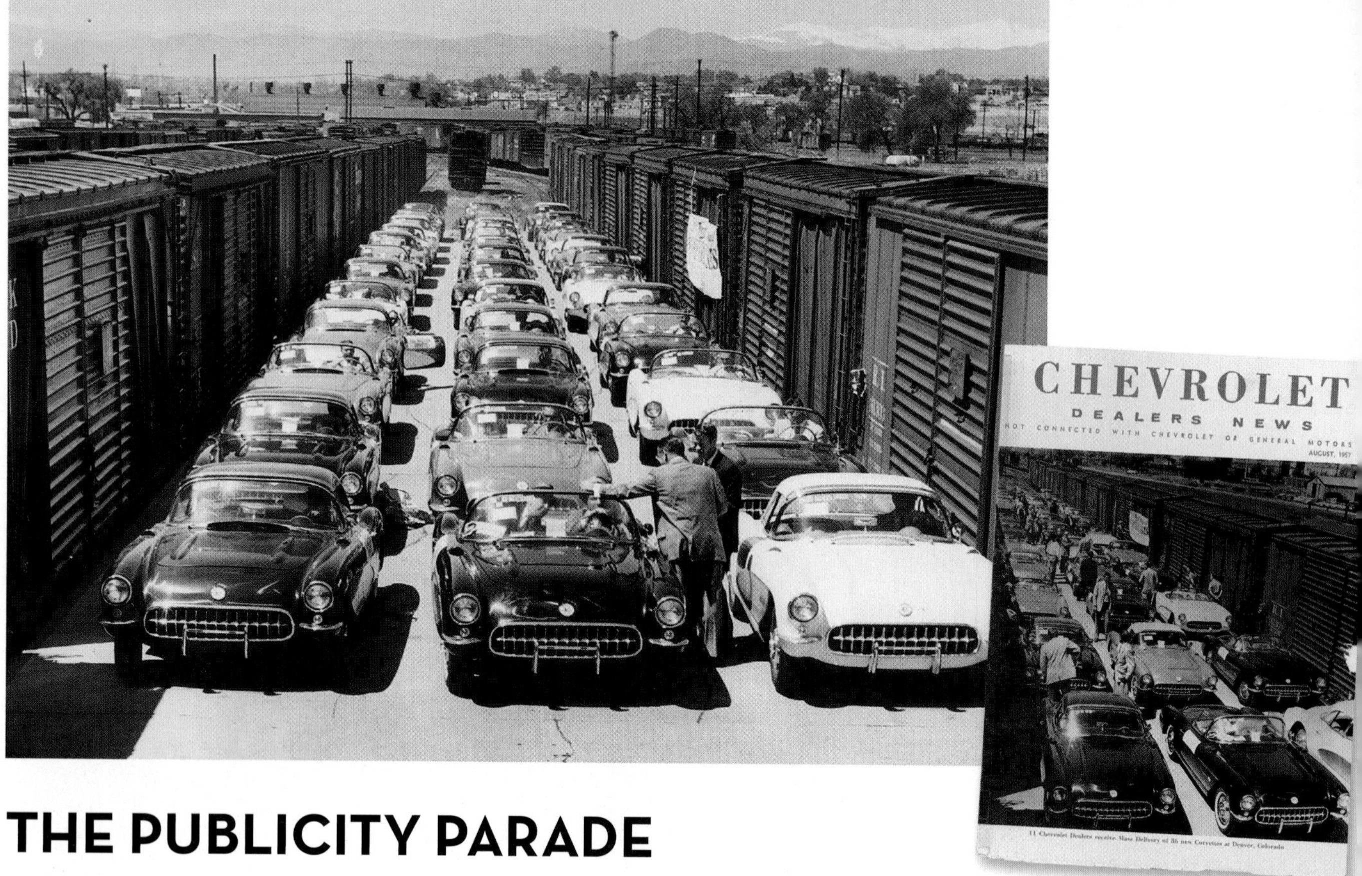

Chevrolet representatives M. C. Lindsey and R. R. Shaw (above) send off a fleet of new Corvettes for a publicity stunt through downtown Denver in 1957.

THE PUBLICITY PARADE

IN 1957, with a new high-performance engine and an optional four-speed manual transmission, the Corvette enjoyed a boost in interest among car buyers. At the time, I was the district manager for Chevrolet in the Denver area.

Looking for a way to capitalize on this new interest, the local dealers and zone managers arranged for a load of Corvettes to be shipped by rail from the St. Louis assembly plant. From the rail yard, they would be driven through the city, attracting the kind of attention that Corvettes usually do—but multiplied, we hoped, by the trainload.

The parade from the rail yard wasn't the easiest thing to pull off. It was a hot August day, so we couldn't drive the cars very fast without overheating. Plus, the carburetors were set in St. Louis and were not quite ready for the mile-high Denver altitude!

All in all, though, things went well, and we got a lot of free publicity from the two Denver newspapers. We even made the cover of the *Chevrolet Dealers News.*

R. R. SHAW • EAGLE, ID

SPEEDING THROUGH TIME

1953
The Corvette prototype debuts in January at the GM Motorama in New York. Later that year, the first production models are made.

1956
Test driver Betty Skelton hits 145.044 mph in her Corvette, setting a women's land speed record in Daytona Beach, Florida.

1962
GM executive Edward Cole presents astronaut Alan Shepard with a Corvette coupe. He appears with it on the cover of *Corvette News.*

1963
Pop band The Beach Boys immortalize the Corvette Sting Ray in their hit "Shut Down," about a drag race between a Dodge Dart 413 and a Vette.

1968
The Hot Wheels Custom Corvette premieres. It's a 1/64th-scale toy version.

1969
Six years after introducing the Sting Ray, GM says the name will be one word, not two.

CORVETTE WAS A CAREER CHANGER

THE FIRST CORVETTE I ever saw was the first Corvette. I was 12 years old when I laid eyes on the prototype in the 1953 GM Motorama road show. Imagine! A born-to-run two-seater with stone screens over the headlights and a body made of fiberglass. Best of all, GM was actually planning to build them. Right then and there I decided I was going to get a Corvette. Little did I know that I would one day help to market them.

In 1966, I sold the worst car I ever owned, a Triumph TR4, and replaced it with the best one I ever owned, a '66 silver pearl Corvette convertible. That same year, the Corvette writer who worked for Chevrolet's advertising agency, Campbell Ewald in Detroit, left for another job. Management needed a replacement—fast. They spotted me, a young punk with less than two years on the job, but one of two people on the Chevy account who actually drove a Vette. So, by 28 years old, I was named the copy supervisor on the Corvette, Camaro and Super Sport group.

As soon as Corvette's sales promotion manager heard the news, he summoned me to his office in the GM building. "Your job is simple," he told me. "We can build 35,000 Corvettes a year. Your job is to create demand for 40,000 Corvettes a year."

I wrote Corvette ads and brochures for the company until 1973. My favorite ad? The autobiographical "If you've wanted a Vette since you were a kid, you've waited long enough."

RICHARD WINGERSON
TALLAHASSEE, FL

Fueled by his own love of Corvettes, Richard Wingerson wrote ads (including those above) for Chevy's advertising agency in the 1960s and '70s.

CLOCKWISE FROM TOP LEFT: R. R. SHAW (2); RICHARD WINGERSON (3); MATTEL, INC.; COURTESY OF GENERAL MOTORS, LLC

1970
Hot rod king George Barris designs the "Foxy Vette" for Farrah Fawcett.

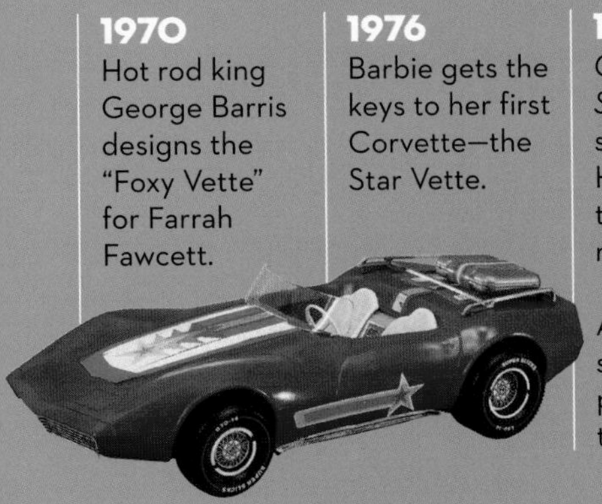

1976
Barbie gets the keys to her first Corvette—the Star Vette.

1978
Corvette Summer, starring Mark Hamill as a teen, debuts in movie theaters.

A Corvette serves as the pace car for the Indy 500 for the first time, celebrating the model's 25th anniversary.

1983
Prince breaks the Billboard Top 10 with his hit single *Little Red Corvette.*

1984
In the movie *Gremlins*, Gizmo saves the day in a pink Barbie Corvette convertible.

1986
NBC airs *Stingray*, starring Nick Mancuso as the driver of a black 1965 Vette.

1994
The National Corvette Museum opens in Bowling Green, Kentucky, near the Corvette assembly plant.

2013
For the car's 60th birthday, Chevy rolls out the seventh-generation 2014 Corvette C7 Stingray.

OPEN-AIR TRAVEL

Warm weather means putting the top down, and that's just the ticket with these sleek convertibles from the 1950s, '60s and '70s. Take a journey through automotive history.

1962

Look! The lid's off Comet

Thousands asked for it...waited for it. And here it is: a convertible by Comet. Wouldn't you know Comet's top-downer would look like this? Racy. Jaunty. Beautiful. It comes in two models including the sporty S-22 bucket-seater (shown) with optional stick shift. And Comet adds to the carefree life with service-savers like self-adjusting brakes. See it, and flip your lid.

'63 MERCURY
COMET

COMET · METEOR · MONTEREY · PRODUCTS OF Ford MOTOR COMPANY · LINCOLN-MERCURY DIVISION

Ford harnessed the power of the 1960s American dream to market the Mercury Comet: beautiful woman, luxury car and a puppy in the back seat.

1972

If ever there were a thoroughbred of cars...

this is it. The Eldorado Convertible by Cadillac. It has the lines, the dash, the spirit. And it has something more. Because this one is unique—even among thoroughbreds. It is the only luxury convertible built in America. The only luxury car with front-wheel drive, Automatic Level Control and an 8.2 litre engine. And you may specify American-made steel-belted radial tires, a Dual Comfort front seat and Track Master skid control. As the convertible or as the classic coupe, it is the world's most elegant personal car. You'll see what we mean when you see your authorized Cadillac dealer to test-drive the Eldorado. This one is a champion.

If ever there were exciting television . . . this is it. The Triple Crown of racing, presented by Cadillac and your Cadillac dealer. The Kentucky Derby, May 6; The Preakness, May 20 and The Belmont Stakes, June 10. Live and in color on CBS-TV. On CBS radio, too. For your viewing and listening pleasure. Cadillac Motor Car Division.

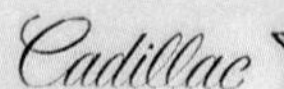

General Motors cleverly synergized with the legendary horse races by creating a Triple Crown of its own: the race to own a Cadillac Eldorado, an Oldsmobile Fiesta and a Buick Skylark.

This beachy Oldsmobile promotion employs the same "rakish lines and bold contours" in its illustration that it boasts in the Classic Ninety-Eight convertible's design.

Lost and Found

A chance drive on a road less taken led an Oldsmobile business coupe back home.

I fully understand how a car can become a real member of a family. We used to own such a vehicle: a 1937 Oldsmobile business coupe. My dad, Henry Bourgeois, bought it from a retired police chief in 1965, when I was about 7 years old.

FAMILY ADDITION

I still remember the day we drove from our hometown of Manchester, New Hampshire, to look at the car. We pulled into a driveway, and there it was: a shiny, cool-looking black coupe with a tall, narrow grille and a long, tapered hood.

Large, rounded front fenders sloped back to the running boards. The rear windows were sleek and curved. The entire car was black except for the chrome grille, bumpers and tiny hubcaps; the wide whitewall tires; and the tan mohair interior.

My father, who collected old cars, took it for a drive with the owner. As a one-owner, low-mileage car, it drove like a dream. When they came back, my father got out and said, "I'll take it!" I was so excited.

For years we enjoyed taking our coupe to car shows and on long weekend drives. Sometimes I'd ride on the back window ledge, with my head against one window and my feet against the other.

I liked to wash and wax it, and on one weekend—with Dad's permission—I even did a little detail painting. The center chrome brake lamp had three lines cast into each side, and I thought they'd look good painted red. My father agreed, and the result was pretty sharp.

EXCHANGE VALUE

The car stayed with us until I reached seventh grade and saw a 1965 Ford M151 Army jeep owned by my social studies teacher. He wanted to sell it, and since I'd liked jeeps ever since I could remember, I had to tell my father about it. My teacher brought the jeep over to our house one day so my father could see it, and during his visit, he spotted our Olds coupe. He really liked it, and before I knew it, we owned a 1965 jeep and my teacher drove away in the coupe.

It turned out to be a poor deal. We had problems with the jeep, while my teacher drove the Olds daily. For years, whenever my father would talk about cars, he'd tell people how he sold the nicest '37 Olds coupe ever and ended up with a junky jeep.

A few times, I even talked to my old teacher about buying back the car, which by that time was in storage. But he declined, and as the years passed, I pretty much gave up on the idea of ever seeing that black coupe again.

WHAT LUCK

All that changed when I took a weekend drive on some New Hampshire back roads in 1979.

I had just glanced back to check on traffic when I saw

Storage time in rented garages kept their beloved 1937 Olds coupe in good shape over the years.

Henry had the car fixed and painted and the interior restored with the original materials after his treasured 1937 Olds came "home."

a familiar-looking black car parked on a front lawn.

I quickly turned around to investigate and couldn't believe my eyes. It was a '37 Olds business coupe and it had a "For Sale" sign on the windshield!

With a pounding heart and sweaty palms, I got out and walked up to the car. How could I tell if this was our beloved little black coupe? Then I remembered those red lines I'd painted in the brake lamp housing. I went around to the back of the car and saw those familiar lines of red paint. This was our old car!

By this time, the man who owned the car had come outside. The coupe didn't look as shiny as it once was, but when started up, the engine still ran well. He asked if I wanted to take it for a test drive, and I agreed, smiling from ear to ear.

When I returned, we settled on a price for the car, which he had bought from my old teacher. I gave him a deposit, and he held it for pickup.

BACK HOME

As luck would have it, Father's Day was just a week away. When I got home and told my mother what had just happened, we decided to pool our money and buy the car to surprise Dad.

For years, he'd tell people how he sold the nicest '37 Olds coupe ever and ended up with a junky jeep.

The Olds was delivered a couple of days before Father's Day, when my dad was away from home. We got it into the garage, closed the door and prayed my father wouldn't go inside.

On Father's Day, Mom and I each gave Dad a small gift and a card, and then told him that one more present was in the garage because it was too big to bring inside. He seemed quite puzzled.

I went in first and turned on the lights. When Dad walked in, his eyes grew as wide as silver dollars. "Wow!" he said. "It's an Olds business coupe, just like the one I used to have!"

And when Mom and I told him it was better than that, he was stunned. He just kept walking around the coupe, repeating over and over, "This is my car."

After a little while, it finally sank in that his little coupe had made its way back home. It was fun telling him how I'd found it.

Dad eventually had the coupe restored and enjoyed it for many years before he passed away. Today, with only 15,000 original miles, our '37 Olds still looks brand new—a fond reminder of my father's love for old cars.

KEVIN BOURGEOIS

NEW BOSTON, NH

'57 CHEVY, ROUND THREE

IN 1962, when my parents brought home a 1957 Chevy Bel Air they'd bought for $700, it was love at first sight for me. I was 15 at the time, and when I turned 18 my brother Bob and I bought the Bel Air from my parents for just $200, because the engine crank had blown. We found another engine for $200 and had someone put it in.

The following year, Bob totaled the Bel Air, but I thank God he wasn't hurt. I went and bought another '57 Chevy two-door, and the owner of the body shop where I worked helped me rebuild it. While I was in the Air Force, Bob and our dad installed the engine I'd bought for it.

When I came home from serving in Vietnam, I was driving my Chevy and someone hit me from the rear and totaled the car. So I went out and bought a '57 Chevy station wagon. It had to be towed home, and Dad wondered what I was going to do with the pile of junk. I said I was going to rebuild it, something I didn't complete until 1977. But I still own it.

So I've had a '57 Chevy since I was 18; now I own eight of them!

LARRY DEMASSE JR.
BRIDGETON, NJ

As family cars go, the Bel Air handed on to Bob (left) and Larry Demasse was a pretty sweet ride.

The Smith twins were proud of their Christmas present in 1957; Lloyd relived the surprise in 2003.

Double the Fun

It was the perfect gift—twice.

This unusual tale of twin cars begins in Oregon on Christmas morning 1957, when my brother Larry and I were 17. The two of us kept opening package after package—all of them empty except for a few notes.

"Not this one," read one. "Nope, not this one," read another. "Maybe the next one."

Finally, we got to a little box holding a set of keys. We all went outside, and there was our present, a new black and yellow Chevy 210.

That car became our daily companion. After we finished high school, we drove it to Longview, Texas, where we both attended LeTourneau University and earned degrees in industrial engineering. We traded it back and forth for years. I drove it while courting the woman who became my wife, Helen.

By 1966, the Chevy had logged more than 120,000 miles. It was worn out, so we sold it for $350, but I kept a photo of it. I had a recurring dream that I was driving it once more.

Years later, Larry and I both became teachers and Helen and I raised three children, Kenneth, Keith and Jeanne.

Unbeknownst to me, my son Keith began plotting in 2002 to find me a twin of that first, much-loved Chevy. He'd hoped to locate the original, but he couldn't trace it.

Instead, he enlisted the help of a friend, who spotted a '57 Chevy in Arizona that looked in near-original condition, though the engine had been rebuilt. Keith bought it, repainted it black and yellow, and replaced the seats.

On Christmas morning 2003, we gathered at my parents' home in Medford, Oregon. Someone handed me a present that contained a note: "Not this one."

"This is shades of 1957," I said.

I opened package after package and, sure enough, the smallest one had a set of keys. We all went outside, and there was my present, a restored 1957 Chevy 210. Tears welled in my eyes as I gazed on it.

All these years later, I still marvel at it and the lengths my son went to give it to me. The Chevy is a beloved part of our family now, and I hope to pass it on to Keith's son Bennett, who enjoys taking it out with me.

LLOYD SMITH · LONGVIEW, WA

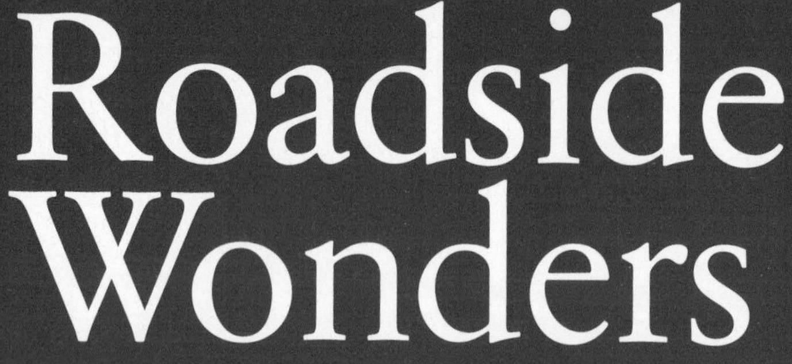

Roadside Wonders

Who didn't beg Mom and Dad to revise a family road trip to include a detour past some offbeat guidebook spectacle?

BY LEAH WYNALEK

CABAZON DINOSAURS

WHERE: Cabazon, CA
BACKSTORY: Intended to lure drivers off the interstate and into the Wheel Inn cafe, the dinosaurs of Cabazon have become a destination in their own right, thanks in part to some memorable movie cameos. Dinny opened in 1964 and Mr. Rex joined in 1981. Today they're the centerpieces of a creationist museum.

PAUL BUNYAN & BABE THE BLUE OX

WHERE: Bemidji, MN
BACKSTORY: Although both were constructed in 1937, the famous lumberjack and his big ox didn't stand together until years later. Bunyan's 18-foot-tall, 2.5-ton likeness was commissioned for the city's Paul Bunyan Carnival, while his 5-ton companion traveled by truck promoting Bemidji. These days the duo attracts thousands of visitors a year to the city that calls itself the *real* birthplace of Paul Bunyan.

THE BLUE WHALE OF ROUTE 66

WHERE: Catoosa, OK
BACKSTORY: Lifelong Catoosa resident Hugh Davis built this oddity in 1972 as an anniversary gift to his wife, Zelta, an avid collector of whales. Before the 80-foot-long structure got its first coat of paint, people began stopping to peek through the holes in its head. Old Blue remains open to curious travelers.

UFO MUSEUM & RESEARCH CENTER

WHERE: Roswell, NM
BACKSTORY: In July 1947, a crash landing put Roswell on the map. A press release issued by officers at the Roswell Army Air Field referred to the recovery of "a flying disk," but the military later called the recovered object a weather balloon. The debate continues. You can do your own research at the museum.

AROUND THE WORLD IN AN AIRSTREAM

Few products—the Coca-Cola contour bottle, perhaps, or the Volkswagen Beetle—are as shapely as the Airstream trailer.

THE SILVER BULLET from Jackson Center, Ohio, was the brainchild of a charismatic businessman named Wally Byam. It has been celebrated for decades as a favorite home away from home.

Now that our kids are grown, our Airstream has a permanent home on 10 wooded acres. It makes for a perfect weekend getaway.

BARB WALKER PRESSLEY

We live in our Airstream as much as we do in our house. We have visited 48 states, four Canadian provinces and too many great parks to count.

RICHARD HUNT

We bought our '71 Airstream 15 years ago from a lady whose husband had passed on. Walking into that trailer was like going into a time capsule, avocado-green shag carpet and all. We always remember that couple as we take our own vacation journeys, vowing never to miss a chance for a trip.

JACKIE PARKER MORGAN

When Wally Byam entered the travel trailer business in 1932, he had fewer than 50 rivals. Five years later he had more than 400—many of them shameless Airstream knockoffs. Today, of that multitude, only Airstream remains.

WALLY'S WORLD

Behind the beloved travel trailer, a brilliant businessman in a blue beret.

WALLY BYAM WAS BORN on July 4, 1896. As a boy, he worked as a shepherd, spending nights in a small two-wheeled donkey cart equipped with a washbasin, a kerosene heater and a sleeping bag. It was a fitting start for the man who would go on to start Airstream.

Byam's first trailer, built in 1929 in the backyard of his Los Angeles home, consisted of a tent erected atop a platform attached to a Ford Model T chassis. It was an unlovable contraption, particularly to his first wife, Marion, who refused to go camping without at least a basic kitchen. So Byam replaced the tent with a teardrop-shaped cabin that included a small stove and an ice chest. He wrote a magazine article titled "How to Build a Trailer for One Hundred Dollars" and earned $15,000 selling detailed construction plans for a buck apiece. He built several more trailers, refining his design with each one, until neighbors began complaining about the noise. So in 1932, Byam rented a proper factory building and called his operation the Airstream Trailer Co.

But his first trailer (above) bears little resemblance to the now-famous silver bullet. Credit for that shape belongs to William Hawley Bowlus. An aircraft designer who had served as foreman in the shop that assembled the Spirit of St. Louis for Charles Lindbergh, Bowlus created a dramatic aircraft-inspired travel trailer made of aluminum. Unfortunately, he proved to be a more gifted designer than he was a businessman, and his company went under after producing just 80 trailers.

Enter Wally Byam, who had done some sales and marketing for Bowlus. He was there to pick up the pieces, and in 1936, shortly after the failure of the Bowlus Trailer Co., Airstream—with former Bowlus workers using former Bowlus equipment—debuted an aluminum wonder called the Clipper. The rest is history.

In the years that followed, Byam (below, wearing one of his signature blue berets) was more than Airstream's chief executive. He was the company's greatest champion, traveling the country—and later the world—with a trailer in tow, building a legend that survives to this day.

EXCEPT AIRSTREAM PARADE: COURTESY OF THE HELEN BYAM SCHWAMBORN ESTATE

Happy Campers

When adventure knocks for these nature lovers, all they have to do is open the door.

The birchwood interior makes the camper warm and cozy without much extra decor.

After my husband's successful battle with cancer in 2011, we found ourselves trying to figure out a new direction for our lives. Vaughn and I had never camped before, but as longtime antiques collectors, we thought a vintage trailer might be a good way to take our passion on the road.

What we ended up with was not your typical trailer but a distinctly different beauty: a 13-foot 1955 Aljoa Sportsman in very good condition. It has basically the entire original birchwood interior as well as the original four-burner stove, gas lamp and icebox!

Now we go on about five trips a season, ranging as far north as Lake Placid, New York, and as far south as Virginia's Assateague Island, where the wild ponies roam. We've been as far east as Montauk Point on our native Long Island and have plans to attend a Civil War reenactment at Gettysburg. We also like to participate in vintage camper rallies each year. Our 3-year-old Boston terrier, Bosco, always comes along with us. He is a good boy and sleeps very soundly in our camper.

I cannot explain the absolute joy we get from waking up in our trailer with the sun shining in, illuminating the wood to a beautiful honey brown, and stepping out to see pine trees and a serene lake. We like to canoe, swim, sit by the lake and take lots of nature photos. Because our trailer is relatively small, we're able to detach the car from it to explore local towns and go to roadside antiques markets and garage sales. But nothing beats sitting in front of our camper and looking up at a sky full of stars.

MERRIE MARTINIAN
MALVERNE, NY

Vaughn and Merrie snap a selfie during a vacation in their little vintage trailer.

MERRIE & VAUGHN MARTINIAN (3)

WINGING IT

From smartly dressed passengers to fancy in-flight meals, air travel was both exciting and glamorous. The jet-setters of yesteryear were eager to fly the friendly skies.

NO REGRETS

To pay for my first plane trip in 1950, with my Rochester, Minnesota, church group, I had to take out a loan. My itinerary included New York City, Paris and Rome. I had the loan paid off in a year, and I'm happy to say I would do it again in a heartbeat. I'm in the first row, second from right.

BETTY BURNS • WAITE PARK, MN

BIG WINNERS!

In 1962, the Sinclair Oil Corp. launched a nationwide contest to see which gas station owner could increase his sales the most. The prize: a three-day, all-expenses-paid trip to Miami Beach. I won! This photo of my wife, Eveleyn, and me was snapped as we boarded the plane.

ED HARBISON • CULLMAN, AL

FLIGHT OF THE HONEYMOONERS

This is my wife and me on the day of our first airplane trip, Nov. 8, 1958. I was 20, and my wife was 19. We flew to Washington, D.C., for three days and then headed up to New York City by train, where we stayed at the Statler Hilton and went to the famous Birdland Jazz Club to listen to Dizzy Gillespie. After the show, he autographed our menu. Years later, I sold that menu on eBay for $375. The entire honeymoon cost $375!

RON FERRARO • WEBSTER, NY

PENNY-A-POUND AIR FREIGHT

I wonder if anyone recalls half-hour airplane rides being offered for 1 cent per pound according to your weight.

In 1939, when I was 8 years old, my father had a surprise for me. At the time, Northwest Airlines had just acquired its first Douglas DC-3s and was sending them around the States to show them off.

We lived in Brainerd, Minnesota, and Dad and I were at the small airport on the south side of town when a DC-3 landed on the single grass airstrip. My father paid 80 cents for me to get a ride, which remains one of the highlights of my life.

It was a special gift from Dad, who might have made only a dollar a day in those Depression years.

BOB CRAWFORD • APPLE VALLEY, MN

BOTTOM RIGHT: JAMES STEIDL/SHUTTERSTOCK

VINTAGE ADS

TRAVELING IN STYLE

In the postwar years, transportation companies were losing vacation dollars to the roomy, go-anywhere family car. These ads encourage the adventurous to head for the sky.

1947

Get your own and fly anywhere! This ad was marketed to both men and women to consider the next step up from owning an automobile: personal plane ownership.

New Stinson Flying Station Wagon

It's here! Stepped up in range, speed, payload!

The great new Stinson for '48

New? Yes! But more important, the new 1948 Stinsons—of *proved* design—are America's most *useful*, most *practical*, personal planes.

For a Stinson carries four people comfortably and economically—is equally useful for family or business travel. Its roomy interiors—newly styled by the famous designer Henry Dreyfuss—provide plenty of luggage space.

Long time fliers prefer Stinson dependability and safety. Beginners are delighted with Stinson flying ease and simplified control. You can learn to fly solo in ten hours or less.

Visit your Stinson dealer for a look at the Stinson Voyager or Flying Station Wagon. See for yourself why Stinson leads in popularity in the 4-place field.

Better yet, arrange with your dealer for a demonstration flight. Then you'll understand why Stinson owners regard personal flying as the most modern, most comfortable, most profitable way of going places!

For literature write Stinson Division, Dept. B, Consolidated Vultee Aircraft Corp., Wayne, Michigan.

For 22 years, builder of America's most useful personal planes

Stinson

New, safer, "Fly-anywhere" performance
Quick take-offs. Short, slow landings. Cruises at 130 m.p.h.—longer non-stop range of 554 miles—at 5,000 feet. Gas and oil costs less than 4c per mile.

New, higher pay-load capacity
640 cargo and baggage pounds plus pilot—or four people with 100 pounds of luggage or cargo. Has side-loading baggage compartment.

New, greater all-purpose utility
28% greater range, 14% more useful load. Can be equipped with floats or skis. Rear seats removable in Flying Station Wagon.

New ease of control, new dual brakes
The spin-resistant Stinson is so easy and safe to fly that beginners usually solo in ten hours or less. Solo flight instruction included in purchase price.

Stinson has new flight instruction plan for business and professional men interested in saving time and money—write W. H. Klenke, Jr., General Sales Manager, Stinson, Wayne, Michigan.

Here I am -- the fellow who said he would never fly!

"If I'd thought it was anything like this, I'd have been flying long ago! Here I am, enjoying undreamed-of travel comforts, seeing beauty I never knew existed, saving *days* of time! It's not costing me a penny more, but I'm sure *getting more!*"

Most everyone who flies has at one time said: "*I'll* never fly!" But wisdom whispered: "Don't be too sure. It's a *big* thing! Better try it and see." And so they flew . . . and alighted from their first flights, elated, discoverers of a new world! You, too, have only to *fly* to know that travel by air is a reality for *thousands* every day and night the whole year around, and that the sooner you adopt flying, the sooner you catch up with other modern-day folks! American Airlines, Inc., Dept. E-20, 20 North Wacker Drive, Chicago.

Serving America's Major Cities From Coast to Coast

1949

It's hard to imagine the days when smoking was still allowed on passenger airplanes, but this ad from 1949 showcases this fact. The suited gentleman seems quite comfortable with a large curtained window and reclining seat.

The passengers at right look like they are at a lounge rather than riding an airplane. The comfort of a smooth ride (with a beverage in hand) was a selling point, more so than wearing a seat belt.

1946

THE SATURDAY EVENING POST

July 13, 1946

The luxurious lower-deck lounge of the Boeing Stratocruiser

Smoothest ride in the world

Aboard a Boeing Stratocruiser you'll experience a new kind of ride—incomparably smoother than you've ever known in surface transportation of any kind—or in any other airplane.

You'll relax and rest completely—go downstairs to the sumptuously appointed lounge—write letters or read—and all the while you'll feel scarcely more motion than in your easy chair at home.

There are good reasons for this amazingly smooth ride. The size of the airplane—the unique Boeing wing and other features of aerodynamic design—the over-weather altitudes at which it can fly—and its speed of more than 5 miles per minute—all contribute to level, velvet-smooth flight. Even air bumps that would be severe in other transports are reduced to a minimum by the Stratocruiser.

The same Boeing engineering leadership that produced the sturdy B-17 Flying Fortress and the great B-29 Superfortress builds both stamina and easy riding qualities into the Stratocruiser. Boeing Airplane Company, Seattle, Washington; Wichita, Kansas.

The Stratocruiser's unequalled speed, comfort and reliability will soon be available on these forward-looking airlines—Pan American World Airways, Swedish Intercontinental Airlines, Northwest Airlines, American Overseas Airlines—for which Boeing is building fleets of these super-transports

BOEING
STRATOCRUISER

THE SATURDAY EVENING POST

SALES GO UP
when Salesmen do!

WHETHER your principal problem is to assure more calls within a given territory or to expand the coverage of individual salesmen, air travel supplies an economical and logical solution.

For, as many alert companies have already discovered, air travel is the only means of transportation that enables you to increase the efficiency of individual effort without increasing the cost. And today, as always, that is the surest path to profit.

Let American's Flagships show you that air travel is *good* business because it *gets* business.

America's Leading Airline **AMERICAN AIRLINES** INC.

1950

Air travel was promoted not only to the vacationers looking to get away, but to businessmen in the 1950s as a way to increase a company's imprint.

1946

Passenger travel overseas to Ireland was marketed in this aerial-view ad as a delightful experience. The opportunity for world adventure was just a phone call away by contacting your local travel agent.

THE WORLD ACCORDING TO FLIGHT ATTENDANTS

In the jet age, formal dress wasn't just for passengers—flight attendants were expected to be prim and polished to deliver you to your destination comfortably and safely.

SERVICE ON SILVER

Meal service was very different when I was a flight attendant from 1954 to 1960. The silver tray I'm holding was heavy with coffee, cream, sugar and mints.

BETTE WELDY BURFIELD
BALLWIN, MO

REGULATION STYLE

In 1961, I was 20, and had graduated from Trans World Airlines Hostess School in Kansas City. I'm pictured here in the bottom row, fourth from right. As flight attendants, our weight and hair length were regulated, and we had to wear makeup and girdles—no jiggling allowed. We were checked often, before and after flights.

SHARON CLINTON • COOS BAY, OR

HOW HIGH IS TOO HIGH?

When Bahamas Airways modernized in 1968, flight attendants were wearing my designs. During a photo op, one attendant caught the eye of photographers—and the ire of company brass. Earlier, she had asked how short they could wear their dresses. I said, "As short as you want, if you have gams that belong on a Folies Bergère runway." Big mistake! Her appearance gave the impression she was wearing nothing but a white jacket. She lowered the hem.

BOB BRIDE • OAKLAND PARK, FL

Bob Bride's original sketches for Bahamas Airways (top); the full outfit (above); Bob Bride posing with a flight attendant (left).

Pedals and Mettle

Keeping his 1936 Columbia bike all these years—and counting!

Though it may seem hard to believe, I own a bike that's been in my family since the late summer of 1943.

That's the year my older brother, Dwight, saved enough money to buy the used 1936 Columbia for $26. Looking back, it was quite a bargain in those days!

At that time, my family lived in New Philadelphia, Ohio. When we moved to Castleton, Indiana, in 1944, the bike came with us. I still remember the times Dwight rode me to the store to get rabbit feed. While he pedaled, I sat on the crossbars, holding the bag over the handlebars and on the front fender. What fun!

Another time, when our well went dry, we rode the bike three blocks down the road to get water, using the same system. How we managed to keep the water from splashing out is beyond me.

Through frequent moves to different houses, the bike was our main form of transportation. Along with our younger brothers, Don and Frank, Dwight and I rode it to jobs, Boy Scout meetings and everything else.

When Dwight started to drive a 1932 International pickup truck, the bicycle finally was mine. I'd tie my saxophone to the handlebars so I could ride my bike to summer music lessons!

As the years flew by, we boys continued to give the bike a good workout. But in 1952, I bought a motor scooter and willed the old bicycle to Don and Frank.

After we'd all grown up and left home, the bicycle stayed with my parents until 1961, when I took it over to my house, riding it when I had the time. I even learned to ride it backward by sitting on the handlebars and looking over the rear tire. That was fun!

But the bicycle was mostly forgotten for about the next 45 years or so as my wife, Linda, and I had our hands full with three boys of our own, as well as raising horses. Eventually, we gave the bike back to Dwight in 2008.

Three years later, Dwight said he needed more room in his garage, so I agreed to take the bike back. I just wasn't ready to see it go after all those years.

I decided to restore it. So I disassembled it piece by piece, then stripped off all the rust and old paint until I could see the bare bones of its metal frame.

I primed everything with three coats of paint, sanding between each coat. For the finish, I applied two coats of black enamel. All the parts are original except the tire tubes, the white sidewall tires, the seat and two bearings for the wheel sprocket.

Now the bike has a brand-new life. I've ridden it several times, but since I'm a little older, too, I haven't tried to ride it backward again—yet.

LARRY MILLER
FOUNTAINTOWN, IN

Larry removed years of rust from the bike and made it ready to ride.

TWO FOR THE ROAD

My grandparents George Zeman and Mabel Miller hopped on his new Excelsior Autocycle in 1914, the year before they got married. My grandfather told me many stories of that bike, and I, too, took up motorcycle riding.

DAN ZEMAN • CENTRAL POINT, OR

JOBS WE REMEMBER

CHAPTER 4

To some of us, work is about bringing home the bacon or simply trying to make ends meet. But if we're lucky enough to love what we do for a living, our jobs provide a sense of pride. Enjoy these accounts of classic professions, a few of which now exist only in history books.

White gloves and a hat were essential attire when Millie became a Gibbs girl.

Secretary Boot Camp

As a Katharine Gibbs girl, she learned typing, shorthand and punctuation, all while wearing high heels and white gloves.

Career choices were very limited for a young woman in the early 1960s. I found secretarial work more enticing than nursing or teaching, and in my senior year of high school, I was selected to attend the best secretarial school of the day: the Katharine Gibbs School. Once my acceptance letter arrived, I was headed to New York City!

My dorm was the Barbizon Hotel for Women. I was in awe the first time I entered the sweeping lobby and surveyed my new home. Katharine Gibbs had reserved several floors of this grand hotel just for its students, as well as a private dining room.

I had my own room, too, with a colorful bedspread and matching curtains. In front of my bedroom window was a desk with a typewriter. After my mother helped me unpack, she went back home to Ithaca, New York, and I was on my own for the first time in my life.

In the following days, the Barbizon became a hive of activity as more girls arrived. Many of them came from other states and were just as dazzled by New York City as I was. It wasn't long before I met a bubbly redhead from Ohio named Connie. We became close friends and fierce competitors.

All of us soon settled into our new routine. Each morning I would put on my business suit and hurry out the door to catch the bus. Classes were held in the upper level of Grand Central Station. As we dashed down the sidewalk, construction workers would shout, "Here come the Gibblets!" We stood out from our peers: We were the only girls our age carrying briefcases.

For lunch, Connie and I would get 15-cent hot dogs from a street vendor and then pie and coffee at Horn & Hardart, the famous automat. After lunch, it was back to class.

When we returned from class, we were in so much pain from our high heels that the minute the bus pulled away we'd take them off and limp to the hotel. But by the end of the year, we could wear them all day without problems.

After dinner came grueling homework. The biggest nightmare was the dreaded typing assignment. If you made a typo, you had to start all over again with a clean sheet. Tears were shed, but we learned to type accurately.

Punctuation lessons became our own private language. We'd say things like, "However, comma 22, I need to wash my hair tonight." We assigned every punctuation mark a rule number. It became an obsession; we couldn't stop ourselves from writing rule numbers over punctuation marks. If you saw a small number written over a comma on a street sign, you just knew a Gibbs girl had been there.

We were trained to be the best of the best, but it wasn't all work. We enjoyed exploring the city and strolling through Central Park. Our favorite spot was Malachy's. The drinking age then was 18, and we all qualified! We spent many happy evenings in that little bar.

The school year ended as the certification process began. This was a series of difficult exams covering everything we had studied. Connie and I whizzed through and were among the first group to certify.

All of a sudden it was over. The homework struggles, the cramming sessions, my giggly friends in my room—I was going to miss it all.

Although there were prestigious employers in New York City, I returned to Ithaca and took my first secretarial job at Cornell University. I've recently turned 70 but continue to work as the registrar at a boarding school.

I've left the typewriter behind but still use shorthand. My students sometimes ask me if I'm writing in a foreign language. When I explain the shapes and swirls, their eyes light up, thinking they can learn this "secret code." They have no idea it takes many hours of practice!

The days of being a polished secretary in white gloves have since faded away, but it was so much fun while it lasted.

MILLIE PIRKO TRIFF • HANCOCK, NY

Above, women attend typing and shorthand classes at the Katharine Gibbs School. At left, the girls are dolled up for a night out. Millie (pictured at far right) and Connie (second from left) attend a dance.

WOMAN WITH TYPEWRITER: THE ADVERTISING ARCHIVES/ALAMY STOCK PHOTO; THIS SPREAD, TYPEWRITER: JILL SELL

QWERTY AS A PICTURE

Typewriters have gone the way of mimeograph machines, but for more than 100 years their familiar *clickety-clack* was the sound of an office at work. Here are a few favorite vintage ads for these mechanical marvels.

THE SATURDAY EVENING POST August 25, 1923

It's more than a *portable*—
it's an UNDERWOOD

BEFORE the first UNDERWOOD PORTABLE was made, more than two million UNDERWOOD typewriters had already gone on duty—speeding the world's business.

When you buy an UNDERWOOD PORTABLE you call to your service all the skill and ability of the men who have produced —two million times over—the recognized *standard* typewriter of the world.

All that is associated with the name UNDERWOOD—which everywhere means typewriter *speed, accuracy and durability*—is embodied in this PORTABLE. Write for descriptive booklet.

PRICE $50 IN U.S.A. WEIGHT 9¾ LBS. CASED.

The Portable is obtainable at Underwood Offices in all principal cities, or direct by mail.

UNDERWOOD TYPEWRITER CO., *Inc.*, UNDERWOOD BUILDING, NEW YORK

UNDERWOOD PORTABLE

Dominant in standard business typewriters, Underwood introduced its portable in 1919. Early ads for the portable catered to traveling businessmen, but by 1923 the company had turned to the home market, while stressing Underwood's professional-grade quality.

THE SATURDAY EVENING POST APR. 12, 1930 115

This ad emphasizes the advantage of owning a Royal Portable Typewriter as a saving grace for those with bad handwriting.

1930

EMBARRASSED BY POOR HANDWRITING?

You will be proud of every word you type on the new Royal Portable

Faster, simpler than you ever dreamed, this improved home typewriter is making writing easy for everyone. So amazingly convenient, so incomparably neat, that even those most proud of their penmanship have been attracted, convinced! To those tormented by poor handwriting it is a most welcome relief! For now they can write with pride and confidence knowing that their every word is a model of impressive legibility.

Try this finest of portables! "Why!" you will exclaim, "I thought I would have to 'learn' and here I am typing as fast as I can write by hand". But this is only a hint of the speed you will attain after a few hours use. And so it will be with every member of the family, young and old. For no sooner is the new Royal Portable in your home than everyone can use it. And they do—from morning till night. Mother's notes and letters, dad's after-hours work, the varied writing duties of the young people—all are typed with new zest and pleasure.

ROYAL TYPEWRITER COMPANY, INC.
NEW YORK CITY
More than 2,000 Royal Portable Dealers in United States

Everyone is praising the new Royal Portable Typewriter. Never have you seen a home writing machine of such beautiful design—with such graceful modern lines, or colors as attractive as its cheerful Duotones. Especially pleasing is the new typeface "Vogue", created to distinguish personal correspondence.

The New ROYAL TYPEWRITER *Portable*

IBM shows a side-by-side comparison of its attractive new typewriter with the striking beauty of a woman. It's simple and to the point.

1953

Letters can be beautiful, too!

IBM Electric Typewriters

INTERNATIONAL BUSINESS MACHINES, 590 Madison Avenue, New York 22, N. Y.
In Canada: Don Mills Road, Toronto 6, Ont.

DID YOU KNOW

Q, W, E, R, T AND Y ARE THE FIRST SIX LETTERS ON THE TOP ROW OF A TYPEWRITER KEYBOARD. MILWAUKEE INVENTOR CHRISTOPHER LATHAM SHOLES DEVISED THE ARRANGEMENT IN THE LATE 1860S FOR HIS NEWFANGLED "TYPE WRITER."

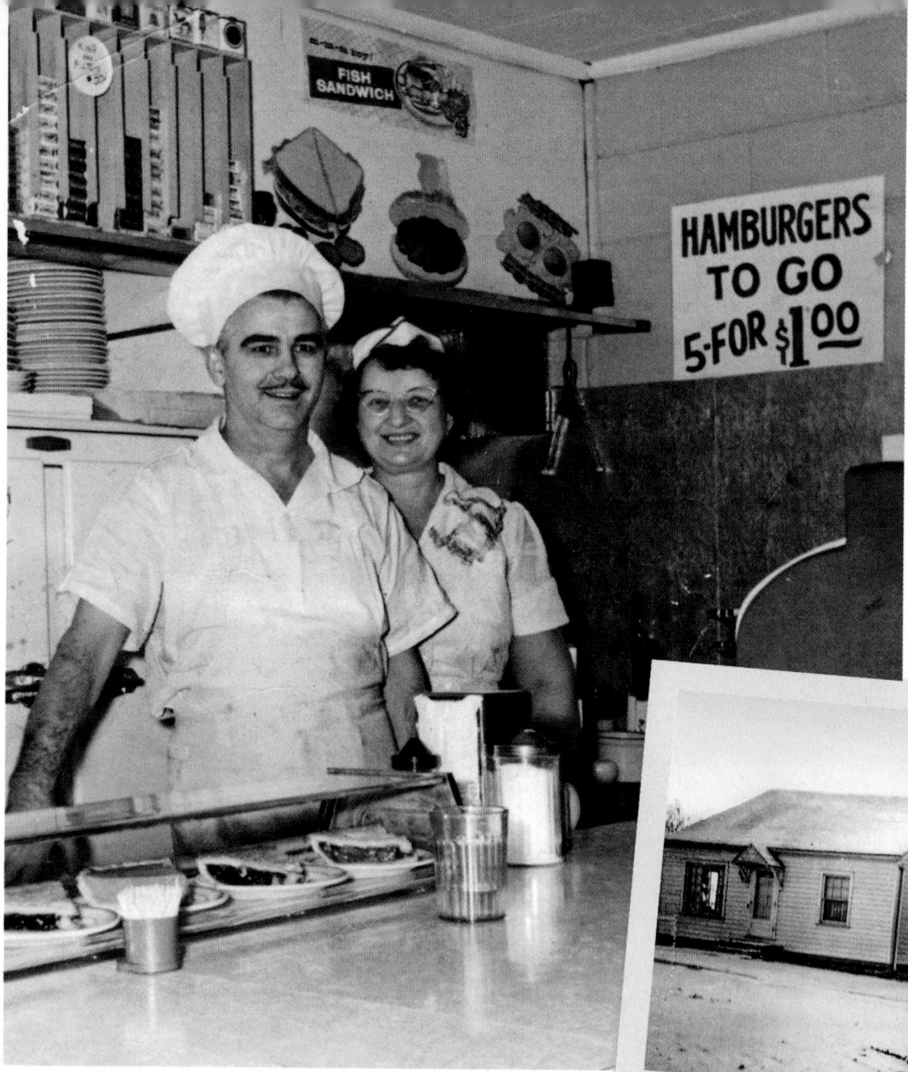

Bill and Louise Stone built a diner next to their house on Route 66.

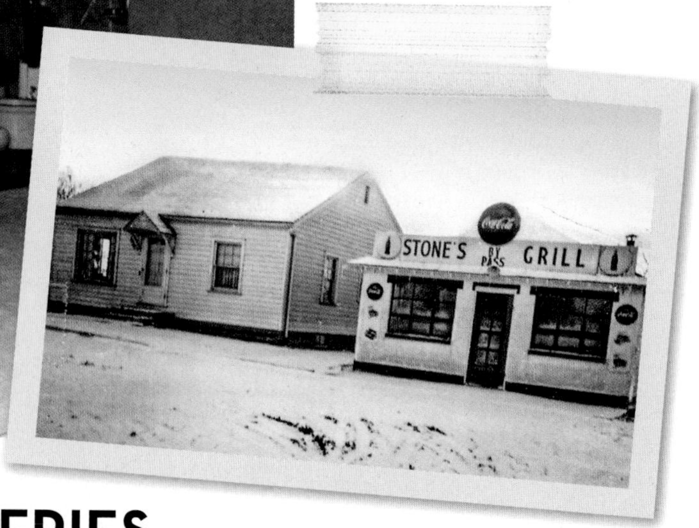

STOP AND SMELL THE FRIES

If traveling the Mother Road, the hungry could get a bite to eat here.

FOR 30 YEARS, from 1946 to 1976, my mom and dad, Louise and Bill Stone, owned and operated Stone's By-Pass Grill in Springfield, Illinois. They bought a house on Route 66 and built the restaurant next door. The route bypassing downtown Springfield is also called North 31st Street or Dirksen Parkway.

Pop modeled his hamburgers after those at Steak 'n Shake. He started with fresh hamburger formed into a ball, then he flattened it on the grill and seared it to perfection.

When we were young, my two brothers and I helped out in the restaurant. My parents taught us to do dishes, wait on customers and peel potatoes for french fries.

The larger potatoes were much easier to peel, so when it was my turn to tackle that particular chore, I hid the smaller spuds. It wasn't long before Pop's profits took a nosedive, while the odor from the back room intensified.

Once my misdeed was discovered, I learned that parental retribution, as it was exercised in 1949, was not to be forgotten. I am certain that Pop's theories of discipline and life lessons have followed me throughout my life.

Thinking back on those bittersweet memories of the 1940s and '50s, I yearn for that gentler and simpler way of life.

ROBERT STONE • HELOTES, TX

TODAY'S THE DAY!
STONE'S BY-PASS GRILL
721 North 31st Street
— Bypass 66 —
Are Celebrating Their ...
10th ANNIVERSARY
Serving Your Favorite Foods Since 1946
• BREAKFAST
• LUNCHES
• DINNERS
Special TODAY
We're Celebrating Our 10th Birthday
WED., MARCH 4, 1959
COFFEE STILL...... 5¢
Hamburgers To Go Out 5 for $1.00
WE FEATURE:
MEADOW GOLD ICE CREAM
— and —
MEADOW GOLD DAIRY PRODUCTS

COOL CATS PASS THE TORCH

One man's jazz is another man's rock 'n' roll.

JUST AFTER I finished college in late 1973 and for the first six months of 1974, I had a job most people my age would have coveted at the time. I worked at The Record Hunter on Fifth Avenue, one of the biggest record stores in Manhattan.

We primarily sold albums. Singles (45s) and cassette tapes were stored behind the front counter, along with accessories—record-cleaning cloths, phonograph needles and blank tapes.

The store was divided into a pop side, which encompassed everything from Sinatra to Led Zeppelin, and a classical side. Both departments had one bin reserved for cutouts, albums that hadn't sold and were now offered at a reduced price.

As with any job, the real story was the people I worked with. Albert, a former refugee from Nazi Germany and the classics manager, watched quietly and saw everything. My immediate manager, Ronnie, had been a teenager during the late '40s and early '50s, and was what we called a jazz cat. Eddie was the third manager.

When I started, I knew about George Harrison, Rod Stewart and Chuck Berry but nothing about jazz musicians. Ronnie took care of that. He introduced me to the giants of the genre: Charlie Parker, Sonny Stitt, Al Cohn and Zoot Sims, Lester Young and others. Soon, he was bragging to Eddie about what a fast learner I was: "Can you imagine that we got a 22-year-old kid who can hum the chart to Benny Goodman's version of 'Sing, Sing, Sing'?"

Ronnie was also a serious Sinatra aficionado. He'd been to 100 Sinatra concerts and had every album Ol' Blue Eyes ever made. He'd also put out a few bootleg Sinatra tapes of his own, which contained radio aircheck demo recordings and studio outtakes not on the albums.

Eddie was a big jazz fan, too, but at 27, much closer to my age. Still, he spoke in 1950s jive talk, saying things like, "A cat digs a chick, a chick digs a cat." He was rail thin with shoulder-length hair and was constantly moving with nervous energy. We talked mostly about the attractive young women who came into the store. On the other hand, he didn't drink, didn't smoke and didn't do drugs. His one weakness was betting at the racetrack.

Those days, record stores were as essential to a young person as a T-shirt, bell-bottomed jeans and a school backpack.

RAANAN GEBERER • NEW YORK, NY

1877 Thomas Edison invents the phonograph, using a stylus to emboss tinfoil wrapped around a cylinder.

1887 Emile Berliner patents the gramophone. The first discs, 5 inches in diameter, were of acid-etched zinc.

1925 The 10- to 12-inch 78-rpm record becomes the industry standard.

1948 Columbia Records introduces the long-playing vinyl record. LPs used finer grooves than 78s and played for 30 minutes a side.

1949 RCA Corp. introduces the 45, or single, a staple for 1950s teens.

Ma Bell on the Line

Switchboard operators connected callers across the board.

Back in the mid-1960s, I was an AT&T telephone switchboard operator in Los Angeles, California.

Our switchboards were rather tall, so we sat on high stools. The headsets we wore originally were uncomfortable because they were so large. Many years later we started using smaller headsets.

We recognized a call coming in when a green light flashed on the board. Then we took a back cord and plugged into the incoming call on the switchboard. When the customer gave us the telephone number they wanted to connect to, we would insert the front cord into a free port and dial the number on a phone dialer on the board.

At 6 each morning, one of our operators would enter a soundproof room and record the weather for Los Angeles Harbor, Catalina, and other seaports.

Holiday workdays were always fun because our office placed calls from the boats in the harbors to landlines. Anyone who was on a boat and had a radio could hear all the conversations. And if there was a party going on with people imbibing alcoholic beverages, the calls could get a little crazy.

Working a switchboard was a wonderful experience. I don't think we truly appreciated our place in communication history, though. Looking back on those years, I have nothing but fond memories of sitting on that tall stool and plugging my headset into the switchboard.

JULIE KALLER • PICO RIVERA, CA

LONG BEFORE SMARTPHONES, EMMA NUTT MADE HISTORY IN 1878 AS THE FIRST FEMALE TELEPHONE OPERATOR. HIRED AWAY FROM HER JOB AT A TELEGRAPH OFFICE BY ALEXANDER GRAHAM BELL, NUTT BECAME THE PATIENT, POLITE VOICE THAT CUSTOMERS OF THE EDWIN HOLMES TELEPHONE DISPATCH CO. HEARD ON THE OTHER END OF THE PHONE LINE. PRIOR TO HIRING NUTT, HOLMES EMPLOYED TEENAGE BOYS, WHO WERE OFTEN BOISTEROUS, CRUDE AND RUDE. NUTT WAS PAID $10 A MONTH FOR 54-HOUR WORKWEEKS. THESE JOBS WERE HELD EXCLUSIVELY BY WOMEN FOR ALMOST A CENTURY.

All lined up on Jan. 27, 1959, to place an average of 50,000 calls per day, these women operated the switchboard on Capitol Hill in Washington, D.C.

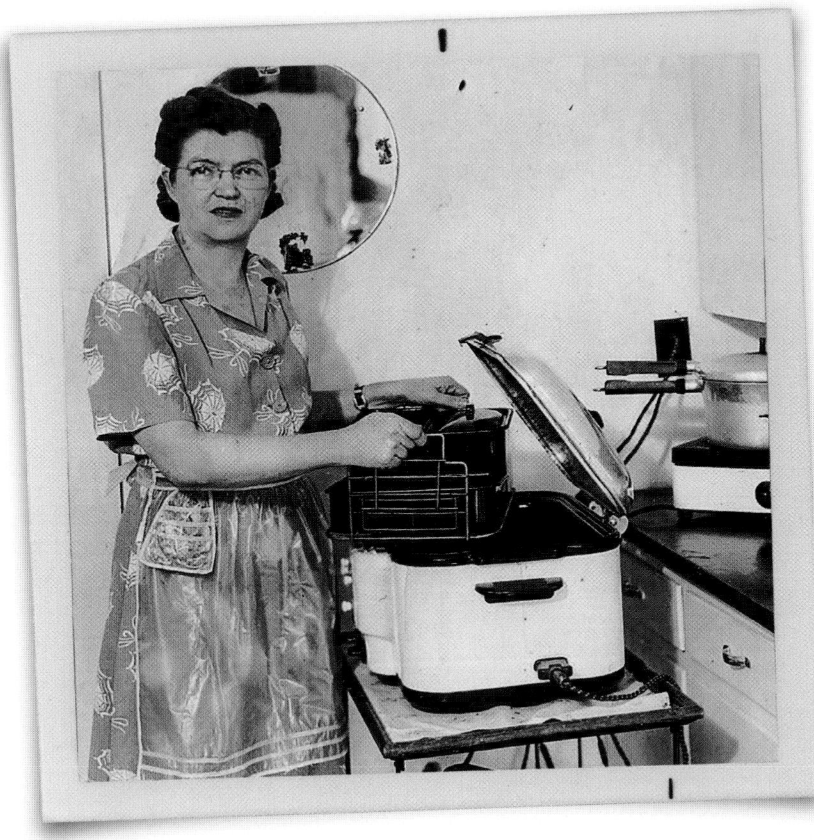

IT'S ELECTRIC!

IN THE LATE 1930s and early '40s, electricity was finally coming to rural northwest Arkansas. My grandmother Edna Henbest was hired by the federal Rural Electrification Administration to contact every rural household in two counties for a study to determine who wanted power lines run to their homes.

The government later hired Grandma to help run a small REA office and to promote the use of electricity by way of home demonstrations. It was pretty much a given that if electric appliances could replace wood-burning cookstoves, the woman of the house would see to it that power came to her kitchen! This picture of Grandma was taken in 1944 in her demonstration kitchen.

ROGER DENNINGTON • LOGANVILLE, GA

SHE LOVED TO STYLE

MY MOTHER-IN-LAW, Lucille Struecker Nelsen, is the young stylist smiling at the camera. This photo was taken at the local beauty shop where she worked. She greatly enjoyed her job and the people she met there.

Please note the contraption in the front of the picture: It was for giving a perm. We laugh now and say it looks like a form of punishment, but at the time, it was the latest method of perming. It certainly puts into perspective how so many things in our everyday lives have changed (and, in this case, for the better!).

My mother-in-law is now in her 80s and lives in a local nursing home. She still notices hairstyles and lets us know what she thinks is a good cut for us!

DIANE NELSEN • RINGSTED, IA

EARNING A LIVING

Hard work never seems to go out of style. Times certainly have changed and many professions along with it, but these workers have what it takes to make it.

HANDWRITTEN TRAVEL

This was taken at General Mitchell Field, the airport in Milwaukee, Wisconsin, in 1959. I am on the left. This is how we made reservations for American Airlines flights—every passenger received a handwritten ticket. Notice there's not a computer in sight!

PATRICIA LYNCH MARKS
GERMANTOWN, WI

ELEGANT BARBERING

My grandfather Henry Hefty, pictured here in the 1920s or early '30s at his barbershop on 32nd Avenue in Denver, Colorado, came to the States from Switzerland in 1886. The door next to the radio led to his living quarters. You can see the photographer's reflection in the mirror. I believe Grandpa had two barber chairs, and he'd put a wooden plank across the arms to seat children, including my sister and me.

EDNA REDDEN • SANTA MARIA, CA

MAKING CONNECTIONS
A trip to Atlantic City, New Jersey, in 1942 for three Jenkintown, Pennsylvania, telephone operators was a great way to make memories. From left are Janet Rubicam, me and Charlotte Kennedy.
BERTHA GIBBONS PITCAVAGE
WINTER SPRINGS , FL

"WELL" DRESSED
From ankle-length aprons to today's colorful scrubs, uniforms sure have changed since my aunts graduated from nursing school in 1920.
JEAN LENDER • MANOR, PA

PAINTING HAZARDS
All the way back on the left is my father-in-law, William Wilson Eccles, holding a spray can. He lost his sight in one eye in a paint accident, and I'd guess it happened while working at this place.
KITTY ECCLES
NESHKORO, WI

Chilly Work, Warm Memories

Before refrigerators became common, this family's ice business helped a Minnesota town keep its cool.

In the late 1930s, my parents, Ed and Verna Spencer, gave up farming. They moved to the town of Bagley, Minnesota, to start Spencer Ice & Dray Co.

While the ice part of the business is self-explanatory, you may not be familiar with the word "dray." In those days, so-called draymen picked up merchandise delivered daily by the Great Northern Railway, then distributed it to businesses in town. They also picked up freight to be shipped.

Draymen also hauled other things, including coal, furniture and trash. But for my family, ice was the main business.

We delivered ice to most of the town's homes and various businesses. Some of my first memories in the early 1940s are of riding through town in a pea-green Chevy pickup, delivering ice to taverns. In particular, I recall Bootsie—the barmaid at Archie Berry's Bucket of Blood, south of the railroad tracks—serving me my first orange soda.

Ed Spencer, the author's father, prepares for a delivery in 1941 by hosing insulating sawdust off 300-pound ice cakes.

Leroy Spencer, the author's uncle, prepares to shovel sawdust into a truck from an immense pile at a sawmill in rural Bagley, Minnesota, in 1942. An effective insulator, sawdust kept ice slabs frozen during storage—even during hot summers.

Keeping Bagley's homes and businesses supplied with ice was a lot of work. First, my dad—with help from his brothers, Leroy and Lawrence, and others—built a two-story icehouse out of tamarack poles and rough pine boards.

There they stored large blocks of ice cut from nearby Lake Lomond. Starting in February, Dad would use a 42-inch circular saw rig that was mounted on skids and powered by a Model A Ford engine to cut the ice into strips to a depth of 24 inches. Then workers used T-handle ice saws to cut the strips into roughly 300-pound blocks, or cakes.

After that, men with pike poles muscled the cakes to what we called an endless-chain elevator, which carried them up to a flatbed truck. There, workers with large tongs would carefully load the cakes, then take them to the icehouse, about a mile away.

It's hard to estimate how much ice we harvested. But there was another ice business in town, and the two operations always produced enough ice to satisfy the whole town's needs until the next ice harvest rolled around. (Keep in mind that back then, people used ice much more sparingly than we do today.)

To keep the ice chilled, icemen used a natural insulation that was available in great quantities: sawdust from a local sawmill. Workers applied a thick layer to the ground floor of the icehouse, and as they stacked the ice cakes, they covered each one with sawdust.

The building had no roof, but even on the hottest summer days, that sawdust kept the ice from melting. Before we made deliveries, we had to hose off all the sawdust.

Dad was a pretty good marketer, handing out cards good for free ice both as a reward to loyal customers and a lure to potential ones. A pink card was good for 50 pounds of ice, and a green one for 25.

Dad and my mom, Verna, operated the ice and dray business until he joined the Army in 1944, at age 33. By the time Dad was discharged

Continued on page 116 ▸

in 1946, refrigerators had rendered ice delivery obsolete. So my parents used a GI loan to open a small general store, and later added a mobile home court.

I still use my dad's ice tongs and a T-handle ice saw to ice-fish for northern pike. And though I'm now in my 70s, the fond memories of my parents' business remain as fresh as the cold, clean ice I helped deliver around town so many years ago.

NOLAN SPENCER
DEERWOOD, MINNESOTA

Spencer Ice & Dray Co. workers unload slabs of ice from a 1938 Chevy truck into the Spencer family's icehouse in February 1942.

Nolan Spencer was 3 years old in the photo above, taken in February of 1942 at his family's icehouse in Bagley, Minnesota. At right, he is with his mother, Verna, and the family delivery truck in 1941.

VINTAGE JOB

GREEN MACHINES

These messenger boys left no carbon footprint.

BACK IN THE DAYS before email, text messaging and overnight FedEx deliveries, smartly uniformed delivery boys—like the ones shown here in downtown Cleveland, Ohio—relied on fleets of sturdy bicycles and pedal power to deliver telegrams and other communications. In fact, accounts of bike messengers date back to the 1870s in Paris.

1 *MR. DEEDS* MAKES DEBUT

These bikes carry signs promoting the film *Mr. Deeds Goes to Town* at the Hippodrome, one of Cleveland's grand old picture palaces. The legendary Frank Capra directed the 1936 comedy starring Gary Cooper and Jean Arthur.

2 RUBBER MEETS THE ROAD

The first bicycle tires were wooden ones reinforced with iron bands. Solid rubber tires followed, which evolved into air-filled by the early 1890s. In 1933, Arnold, Schwinn & Co. introduced balloon tires with inner tubes.

3 DAVID TAKES ON GOLIATH

Irish immigrant John Mackay, who made a fortune from the Comstock Lode silver find during the 1850s, founded the Postal Telegraph Co. in the 1880s to compete against the giant Western Union Telegraph Co.

4 COME FLY WITH ME

In 1936, American Airlines (note poster in window) revolutionized air travel with the Douglas DC-3. The roomier and more comfortable plane helped boost business from 474,000 passengers in 1932 to 1.2 million in 1938.

5 MORE WINDOW SHOPPING

Big plate glass windows were prohibitively priced until the 1860s, when water and steam power made it easier to grind and polish the glass. By 1900, American plate glass was able to compete with Europe's.

These boys worked for the Postal Telegraph Co., where my father worked as an office manager until about 1938 or 1939. The photograph was taken in 1936. The office also had a marching band that took part in local parades.

BOB GAZSO • NORTH OLMSTED, OH

VINTAGE ADS

ENCYCLOPAEDIC MEMORY

Its collective wisdom will carry on in digital form, but the 32-volume print edition of the 244-year-old *Encyclopaedia Britannica* is no longer.

In addition to book-a-month offers like this one from 1957, *Encyclopaedia Britannica* employed upwards of 2,000 door-to-door salesmen, who earned a commission of $500 to $600 for each set they sold. The company abandoned door-to-door sales in 1996.

Now available . . . direct to you from the Publisher

BRAND NEW EDITION OF THE WORLD FAMOUS

ENCYCLOPAEDIA  BRITANNICA

Honor Students use Britannica for Homework!

Britannica makes your home the most interesting place in the world!

Britannica contributes to prestige and business success!

1957

You Get All 24 Volumes Now... Pay Later

On Easy... Book a Month Payment Plan

■ Yes, the latest edition of Britannica—the greatest treasure of knowledge ever published—is now being offered on a remarkable, direct-from-the-publisher plan that puts this world-renowned reference library within reach of *every* family. All 24 volumes will be placed in your home NOW . . . you pay for it *later* on convenient budget terms. It's as *easy as buying a book a month.*

You may wonder how we're able to make this truly amazing offer. First, because of the great demand for this magnificent set, we have ordered a tremendous printing. This enormous printing materially reduces our costs and, under a remarkable *direct-from-the-publisher plan*, we pass these savings on to you.

Thousands of Subjects of Practical Value

In the brand-new edition of Britannica, you will find thousands of subjects that you and your family will refer to in the course of your normal day-to-day affairs. For example, you'll find special articles on household budgets, interior decorating, medicine and health, home remodeling, child care, adolescent problems, rules and regulations for all sports, every kind of hobby . . . plus a treasure house of knowledge on all subjects. Useable information that can save you many dollars.

New Edition is Profusely Illustrated

The new Britannica almost "televises" the information to you by means of 23,494 magnificent illustrations. But it does not merely show "attractive" pictures—it is the work of 5,565 of the world's greatest authorities on all information significant to mankind. Our free Booklet will show you how Britannica presents the accumulated culture of the world in clear, easy-to-read language and superb illustrations. It is the largest and most complete reference set published in America—containing over 38,000,000 words. Its accuracy and authority are unquestioned—it is even offered as evidence in courts of law.

Knowledge Opens the Way to Financial and Social Success

The brand-new Britannica—the biggest and greatest edition in our almost 200-year publishing history—is expressly designed to help *you* enjoy a richer and fuller family life, aid you in achieving greater financial rewards and success in your business or trade, help your children in school, and enable you to speak factually and intelligently on the widest range of subjects.

Yes, Britannica will assure every member of your family the constant companionship of the world's greatest minds. It will enable parents to work more closely with their children at home—helping them build a more solid foundation in today's highly competitive society. Leading educators say: "Too many parents leave the entire educational job up to the school teachers."

Exciting Brochure Now Available

Simply fill in and mail the coupon today, and we will send you . . . *without cost or obligation* . . . a copy of our beautiful, new booklet which contains an exciting preview of the latest edition of Encyclopaedia Britannica. Send no money—not even for postage. It's yours, *absolutely free!*

Act Now to Get Your FREE Booklet in Full Color

In its pages, you will see the most magnificent scenery on the North American continent. You'll go on a cruise to France—to the mysterious Orient—to a Pacific island—or by rocket to the moon! In color so beautifully etched, it gives the illusion of a third dimension, you will see art treasures of famous museums, world landmarks . . . and scientific wond you'll find stimulating material in m of knowledge—presented in the most ing and informative manner possible.

Just as soon as we receive your c will send your illustrated, free bookl you can read and enjoy it at your leis privacy of your home. There is no obl course. However, since this offer is limited, please mail the coupon *toda* slips your mind.

Mail Coupon Now for FREE BOOKLET

along the road of adventure... come with BRITANNICA

ENCYCLOPAEDIA BRITANNICA, DEPT. 205-G
425 N. Michigan Avenue, Chicago 11, Illinois

Please send me, *free and without obligation*, your colorful Preview Booklet which describes the latest edition of ENCYCLOPAEDIA BRITANNICA in exciting ful include complete information on how I may obtain this magnificent set, *direct from* on the Book a Month Payment Plan.

Name ____________ (please print)

Address ____________

City ____________ Zone ______ State ______

In Canada, write E. B. Ltd., Terminal Bldg., Toronto, Ont.

Published in Edinburgh, Scotland, in 1768-71, the first *Britannica* was 2,500 pages and three volumes long, with 160 copperplate engravings.

Grandma Grace took her suitcase as she drove door to door.

Everybody Had to Buy Hosiery

Earning four cars was a bonus!

My grandmother Grace Mills Wilber sold silk hosiery door to door in Dallas County, Iowa, for Wilknit Hosiery Co. of Greenfield, Ohio. As the wife of a farmer and carpenter and the mother of two young boys during the Depression, she did what she could to earn extra income.

She was so good at her sales job that she earned her first new car in 1931. Over the years, she earned three more. In fact, she was such a good saleswoman, an ad with her name in it appeared in the *Woman's Home Companion* in November 1938. Under the headline "Wives HAVE MONEY of YOUR OWN!" the copy read: "Take orders full or spare time like Grace Wilber, who earned $37.10 in 9 hours."

The first car she won was a Model A Ford. Several years ago, when I saw a similar car for sale on a lot in the small town near where I live, I knew I had to purchase it in memory of my grandmother. Everything about the car was original, and my plans include not updating a thing.

I was only 5 when Grandma Grace died, but I love having a reminder of her that I can use these many years later.

CANDACE HORCH
WOODINVILLE, WA

FROM SILK TO SYNTHETIC

1920s

As hemlines rose, every respectable woman donned stockings, preferably silk. Rayon, cotton and wool were poor substitutes.

1930s

The U.S. imported four-fifths of the world's silk, 90% of it coming from Japan, and women's hosiery accounted for about 80% of its use.

1935

DuPont invented a synthetic fiber initially called fiber6-6, later renamed nylon.

1939

Nylon stockings debuted at the New York World's Fair with nylon-wearing models strolling the fairgrounds.

1940

When the silklike stockings went on sale to the public in May, 4 million pairs sold in just days.

1941

After the U.S. entered World War II, nylon's use was restricted to making parachutes, tow ropes, flak jackets and other war-related items.

1945

With the war over, production was slow to rebound. Nylon riots broke out when women lined up for more than a mile to snag at least one of the limited pairs available.

I became friendly with the locals—they tipped better once they got to know you.

For the Good of the Family

In 1939, when I was 14, my family wasn't doing too well. Pop was often out of work or gone for weeks seeking it. Mama and my younger brothers, Earl and Donnie, were doing what they could to earn a nickel.

I had just completed the eighth grade and was looking forward to high school. But there didn't seem much sense in attending school while everyone was starving at home. As sad as it made her, Mama agreed that I needed to quit school and find work.

A friend of mine had an older sister who was employed as a carhop waitress at a drive-up restaurant in Lewisville, Texas. She made $7 a week plus tips. For $1 a week, the owner, Mrs. Langford, would rent the waitresses rooms on the premises set up specifically for her female employees.

My friend said there was an opening for a new carhop. With the little money we could scrape up, I caught a bus to Lewisville the next morning, and sure enough, Mrs. Langford hired me that afternoon. I worked six days a week, except for Sundays, when all the girls would go to church, which was a house rule. I sent $5 a week home to Mama and took the bus back every third Sunday. Mrs. Langford was good to us, charging only half price for anything we ate and taking our letters to the post office for us.

I was on my feet from 10 in the morning to 9 o'clock each night, but I made fast friends with the other carhops and became friendly with the locals who ate there. They tipped better once they got to know you, and I was able to send home a little more each week.

I stayed for two years, until Earl and Donnie were old enough to start working at a local garage fixing cars. They were earning $20 a week between them, so I gave my notice, said my tearful goodbyes, and returned home to help Mama.

There is something to be said for being able to help out your family. When I look back, it may have seemed unfair to some about me missing out on a formal education, but I think it was a fair trade for the welfare of my family.

CYNTHIA HOLBROOK • QUITMAN, TX

HOT DOGS AND FROGS: ANOTHER NIGHT AT THE MOVIES

I HAD A LOT OF DUTIES each night in my first job, which was at San Diego's South Bay Drive-In theater in 1965.

The first was to sell tickets. We were supposed to watch out for cars that had people hiding in the trunk—a clue was a vehicle with just a driver and an apparent heavy load in the rear. But management wanted us to move cars in quickly, giving everyone time to get to the snack bar before the picture started. So we missed a lot of folks in trunks. Most of them ended up buying food and drinks in the snack bar anyway—and that was where the theater made money.

When I worked the snack bar, I could eat anything that was not packaged, such as hot dogs and french fries. If I wanted coffee or soft drinks I had to bring my own cup. The snack bar was near some fields, so occasionally we had an invasion of tiny frogs. We had to keep them from jumping into the french fry grease.

Sometimes a car's occupants were too busy making out to notice that one of them had put a foot on the brake. The bright lights made it difficult for people in the cars behind to see the screen. I'd have to knock on the window and say that I didn't care what they were doing, "just please keep your feet off the brake."

The manager of the South Bay Drive-In at the time, Mark Modine, lived with his family in a mobile home park behind the theater. His son Matthew Modine became the actor who went on to star in dozens of movies, including *Full Metal Jacket, Married to the Mob* and *Pacific Heights*.

The South Bay is still there—one of only two drive-ins left in the San Diego area.

GEORGE GILLOW · BONITA, CA

A salad turned out to be Tammy Finn's undoing while waitressing in a resort restaurant much like this one.

Cool as a Cucumber

Poor salad skills got her chopped from her first summer job.

The summer after my freshman year of college in 1959, I became a waitress at a resort in Rockport, Massachusetts. The salary was infinitesimal, but I figured I would work hard and earn a lot of tips to make up for it.

What the owner didn't tell me was that guests tipped only at the end of their stay, or sometimes not at all. I wasn't going to make much money this summer.

It was the first time I lived away from home. With no car and nowhere to walk to, I spent most nights alone, reading or crying.

Meanwhile, all my college friends were having a ball working and partying at big resorts in New Hampshire and Vermont. They made sure to send me postcards about the fun.

But deliverance was close at hand. Three weeks into June, the owner decided there was insufficient business for three waitresses. Somebody had to go.

It all came down to the salads. Each waitress made her own for each person she served. We had only paring knives to peel the cucumbers, and I had no experience peeling vegetables, so most of the cuke was lost in the process. I was throwing away more than I put in the salad bowls.

When the owner decided that my wasteful cutting was a good enough reason to let me go, I cried. I'd never been fired before.

But frankly, I was relieved to be a failure. I called my boyfriend to pick me up and deliver me from my prison. I cried all the way home, though my tears were tears of anger.

One lasting result of that terrible summer is that I'm probably the biggest tipper around. I have a lot of respect for waitstaff—I'd never attempt that job again!

TAMMY FINN • YORK, ME

LEFT: ARCHIVE FARMS INC/ALAMY STOCK PHOTO

WHAT'LL IT BE?

Running a diner was a short-lived career. My mother, Charlotte Snyder, left, and her friend Mrs. Bimson (I never knew her first name) took out a lease on the basement cafeteria diner at the State Capitol in Cheyenne, Wyoming, early in 1950. They ran it for a few months until my father became ill and Mom got a different job. The cafeteria wasn't making money.

GERRY L. PATTERSON • CODY, WY

THAT'S ENTERTAINMENT

CHAPTER 5

The advent of radio, movies and television—what a time to live! We've come a long way, but we still love to listen to radio programs, get lost in a good movie or share a favorite TV show with family and friends.

The Music that Gave Her Goose Bumps

I grew up singing, dancing to and loving the music of the '40s—Big Bands and swing music. My favorite singer was Frank Sinatra. His crooning gave me goose bumps.

I also loved the music of Benny Goodman, Glenn Miller, Tommy Dorsey, Artie Shaw, Harry James and many others.

Never a wallflower, I jitterbugged and waltzed until the balls of my feet burned, and I limped home. So as a freshman at the University of Arizona, I went with girlfriends to Saturday night dances given for airmen stationed at the training bases in and around Tucson, such as Davis-Monthan, Ryan and Marana airfields. It was a patriotic duty we definitely enjoyed.

I still find it hard to believe that, some years later, my husband and I entertained Benny Goodman in our home. He was a delightful guest and even brought his famous clarinet. After dinner, he played in a trio with another guest, the professor of clarinet at the University of Arizona, and my husband, who was principal clarinetist in the Tucson Symphony Orchestra. What a special treat for our dinner guests.

JEANNE PAFFORD GLASGOW
TUCSON, AZ

Jeanne Pafford with Jim Glasgow, the airman she danced with and later married.

TODAY'S TOP TUNES, RECORDS, ALBUMS

The Billboard
The Music-Record Industry's Leading Newsweekly

Compiled from The Billboard Best Seller Charts

including BEST SELLING Country & Western, Rhythm & Blues

VOL. 8—No. 23

Printed in U.S.A. Copyright 1958, The Billboard Pub. Co., Cincinnati, Ohio

THE HOT 100

First With the Most

☆THE STAR PERFORMER designation shows the outstanding upward changes of position in the HOT 100 or new titles which entered the chart at an unusually high position.

THREE WEEKS AGO	TWO WEEKS AGO	ONE WEEK AGO	THIS WEEK	★ STAR PERFORMER THIS WEEK	TITLE Artist, Company, Record Number	WEEKS ON CHART
1	1	1	1		IT'S ALL IN THE GAME	11
16	5	2	2		IT'S ONLY MAKE BELIEVE	8
13	3	4	3		TOPSY II	11
17	8	3	4		TOM DOOLEY	6
2	2	5	5		ROCK-IN' ROBIN	14
11	10	10	6		CHANTILLY LACE	14
9	9	8	7		TEA FOR TWO CHA CHA	10
7	11	11	8		THE END	8
4	7	6	9		TEARS ON MY PILLOW	13
3	4	7	10		BIRD DOG	14
40	16	15	11		TO KNOW HIM IS TO LOVE HIM	7
5	6	9	12		SUSIE DARLIN'	13
70	21	23	13	★	I GOT A FEELING	4
—	86	18	14		LONESOME TOWN	3
78	44	31	15	★	QUEEN OF THE HOP	5
27	17	21	16		MEXICAN HAT ROCK	8
29	22	19	17		PUSSY CAT	6
6	12	14	18		VOLARE (Nel Blu Dipinto Di Blu)	14
62	35	12	19		FORGET ME NOT	6
10	14	16	20		NEAR YOU	12
8	13	13	21		LITTLE STAR	14
46	28	33	22	★	CALL ME	6
15	15	17	23		YOU CHEATED	11
25	27	26	24		THE DAY THE RAINS CAME	7
61	33	36	25	★	THERE GOES MY HEART	8
79	53	47	26	★	HIDEAWAY	7
18	24	25	27		HOW THE TIME FLIES	12
20	29	30	28		FIREFLY	9
41	36	22	29		THE TEN COMMANDMENTS OF LOVE	8
—	—	67	30	★	THE DAY THE RAINS CAME	2
23	26	28	31		FOR MY GOOD FORTUNE	7
—	72	38	32		A LOVER'S QUESTION	3
83	65	49	33	★	THE BLOB	6
12	23	20	34		SUMMERTIME BLUES	14
76	47	43	35		NEED YOU	5
52	34	34	36		WITH YOUR LOVE	6
55	46	27	37		TOPSY I	8
19	25	42	38		DEVOTED TO YOU	13

TRACKING BILLBOARD'S HITS

While cleaning some things out of my mother-in-law's house, I came across some 1958 pamphlets: "Today's Top Tunes, Records, Albums" from *The Billboard*, the weekly publication tracking the top sellers of the week in what has become known as the Billboard charts. The Hot 100 debuted in the middle of that year.

The pamphlets came from Offermann's, a music store in Saugerties, New York. In my younger days, I picked up the same ones from G.E. Murphy's music store on the town square of Hartford City, Indiana.

The last page of each four-page pamphlet has a place for your mailing address and a stamp to place an order with the record store. In all of them, there were still certain records being offered in 78 rpm versions.

I was 9 years old in 1958 and bought my first 45 rpm records that year; my first 33 rpm album came into my collection a couple of years later.

For me, these pamphlets bring back not just the great music of my youth but the recollections of Hartford City's town square, the courthouse, the World War II monument with my grandpa's name on it and the annual downtown fall street fair. Good times, good memories.

BILL PARKS • KEYSTONE HEIGHTS, FL

SAY! WHAT'S PLAYING?

In 1937, when a broken ankle kept me wheelchair bound for most of the summer, the radio became my constant companion. I was 12, and my new friends included *Oxydol's Own Ma Perkins*; *Our Gal Sunday* (can a girl from a little mining town find happiness as the wife of a wealthy Englishman?); *Stella Dallas* (her daughter Lolly was a pain!); *The Air Adventures of Jimmie Allen*; *Jack Armstrong, All-American Boy*; and *Five Star Final* (with a tough city editor). Other favorites were *Music Appreciation Hour*, all explained by Walter Damrosch; *The Passing Parade* (with John Nesbitt); *Lux Theater* (Jim Ameche and Barbara Luddy); *The Green Hornet*; *Mr. Keene, Tracer of Lost Persons*; *Lum & Abner* (the Jot 'Em Down store); *Amos 'n' Andy* (Kingfish & Ruby, and Sapphire); *Joe Penner* (wanna buy a duck?); *The Bell Telephone Hour*; *Major Bowes Amateur Hour*; and *The Camel Caravan*.

ERNEST PRATT
SANTA BARBARA, CA

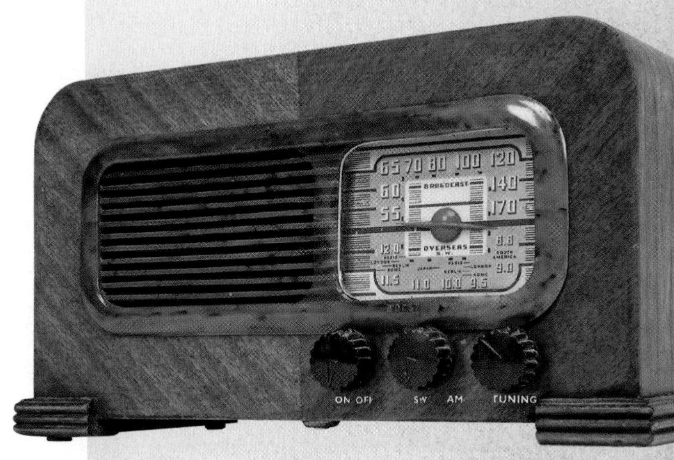

COLLECTION; THIS SPREAD, RADIO: INDEPENDENT PICTURE SERVICE/ALAMY STOCK PHOTO

VINTAGE ADS

TOE-TAPPING FUN

Before iPods, CDs or cassettes, the best way to hear the catchiest tunes of the day was over the radio or on vinyl. Turn your dial back to these vintage ads for radios and records.

The ad at left is dated right before Valentine's Day 1946, promoting Decca Records with lovers and love songs, like Bing Crosby's "The Sweetest Story Ever Told."

1946

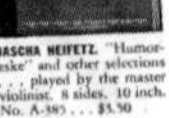

This ad features Nipper, the dog that became an icon for RCA marketing. He was a real dog living in the late 1800s.

1946

A mere six years before Bill Haley's seminal hit "Rock Around the Clock," this RCA ad seems to anticipate the always-on culture of rock 'n' roll, which was helped along by the portable radio.

The beautiful tone and styling of this radio unit are emphasized by an elegant woman standing nearby. Bendix touts the piece as "distinguished enough to become the focal point of any room."

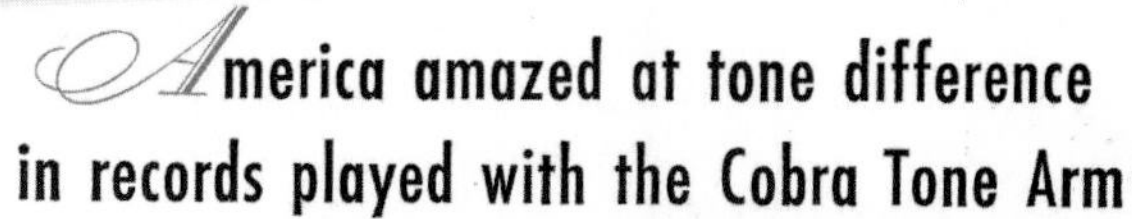

Americans were looking for quality sound even in 1947, as this ad for a radio-phonograph unit from Zenith Radio suggests.

ROCKING OUT WITH CASEY KASEM

The beginning of a new era for American radio stations started with these 40 songs.

ON JULY 4, 1970, disc jockey Casey Kasem launched *American Top 40* by counting down the Top 40 hits each week from the *Billboard* magazine charts (the "40" represented the number of singles that could fit in a jukebox). By the '80s, Kasem's voice could be heard on more than 500 radio stations. Here are the songs he played on that first show:

40. "The End of Our Road"
MARVIN GAYE

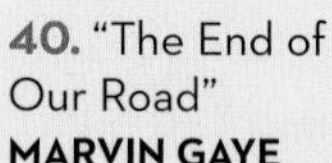

39. "Silver Bird"
MARK LINDSAY

38. "Spill the Wine"
ERIC BURDON & WAR

37. "Go Back"
CRABBY APPLETON

36. "I Just Can't Help Believing"
B. J. THOMAS

35. "Spirit in the Dark"
ARETHA FRANKLIN

34. "Mississippi"
JOHN PHILLIPS

33. "Westbound #9"
FLAMING EMBER

32. "It's All in the Game"
THE FOUR TOPS

31. "Save the Country"
THE 5TH DIMENSION

30. "Ohio"
CROSBY, STILLS, NASH & YOUNG

29. "Everything Is Beautiful"
RAY STEVENS

28. "Check Out Your Mind"
THE IMPRESSIONS

27. "Question"
THE MOODY BLUES

26. "Signed, Sealed, Delivered"
STEVIE WONDER

25. "Sugar Sugar"
WILSON PICKETT

24. "Teach Your Children"
CROSBY, STILLS, NASH & YOUNG

23. "Which Way You Goin' Billy?"
THE POPPY FAMILY

22. "Love on a Two-Way Street"
THE MOMENTS

21. "Mississippi Queen"
MOUNTAIN

20. "Make It with You"
BREAD

19. "Are You Ready?"
PACIFIC GAS & ELECTRIC

18. "Love Land"
CHARLES WRIGHT & THE WATTS 103RD STREET RHYTHM BAND

17. "Tighter & Tighter"
ALIVE AND KICKING

16. "My Baby Loves Lovin'"
WHITE PLAINS

15. "A Song of Joy"
MIGUEL RIOS

14. "United We Stand"
BROTHERHOOD OF MAN

13. "Get Ready"
RARE EARTH

12. "Ooh Child"
THE FIVE STAIRSTEPS

11. "Gimme Dat Ding"
THE PIPKINS

10. "Hitchin' a Ride"
VANITY FARE

9. "The Wonder of You"
ELVIS PRESLEY

8. "The Long and Winding Road"
THE BEATLES

7. "Close to You"
CARPENTERS

6. "Lay Down (Candles in the Rain)"
MELANIE

5. "Band of Gold"
FREDA PAYNE

4. "Ride Captain Ride"
BLUES IMAGE

3. "Ball of Confusion"
THE TEMPTATIONS

2. "The Love You Save"
THE JACKSON 5

1. "Mama Told Me Not to Come"
THREE DOG NIGHT

PARADE OF MEMORIES

IN 1950, I was 8 years old when *Your Hit Parade* first appeared on black-and-white television. On each show, songs were played in an order that led up to the No. 1 hit in America for that week. Many talented vocalists performed regularly. My favorites were Snooky Lanson, Dorothy Collins, Gisele MacKenzie, Russell Arms and Ben Wain.

The series went off the air in 1959, but it provided me with great memories of wonderful music from the '50s. I'm thankful to have experienced it.

ALAN GARFIELD • ESTERO, FL

Here's a list of the tunes that held the No. 1 spot for the most weeks:

10. "If" (19 weeks)
9. "Now Is the Hour" (19 weeks)
8. "Buttons and Bows" (19 weeks)
7. "Peg o' My Heart" (20 weeks)
6. "A Tree in the Meadow" (21 weeks)
5. "Some Enchanted Evening" (21 weeks)
4. "Too Young" (22 weeks)
3. "Because of You" (23 weeks)
2. "I'll Be Seeing You" (24 weeks)
1. "White Christmas" (38 weeks)

TV vocalists Snooky Lanson, Russell Arms, Dorothy Collins and Gisele MacKenzie from *Your Hit Parade*.

RIGHT: ARCHIVE PL/ALAMY STOCK PHOTO

Betty snapped this photo of Elvis signing autographs after his show at the Polk Theatre.

ALL SHOOK UP!

MANY YEARS AGO, Elvis Presley almost started a family feud when my husband, Vic, and I went to see the hip-shaking sensation with Vic's sister, Merle, and her husband, Ed, in 1956.

For a whopping $1.50 each, we bought tickets to The King's 9 p.m. performance at the Polk Theatre in Lakeland, Florida. Neither Vic nor Ed wanted to see "that weird guy wiggle his hips in front of a bunch of screeching teenagers." But when Merle and I said, "That's fine, we'll go alone," they both got in the car and grumbled all the way.

When Elvis finally stepped out from behind the velvet curtain for his 15-minute set, the crowd went wild—except Vic and Ed, of course. Our party-pooper husbands sat with their arms folded across their chests, rolling their eyes.

As Elvis started singing his first song, "Don't Be Cruel," the theater erupted into a frenzy of yelling, arm-waving women. Merle and I clapped wildly with the kids, but Ed and Vic snorted and squirmed in their seats, saying, "Let's get out of here!"

During the second song, "Love Me Tender," we could hardly hear Elvis' crooning over the screams and sobbing. By then, Merle and I were teary-eyed and on our feet, stretching our necks to get a better look at Elvis the Pelvis. By song's end, we were shouting our approval with the rest of the crazy fans.

"Sit down and act your age," Ed hissed, pulling Merle's hand. Vic tugged on my shirttail and said something, too, but I just ignored him and watched Elvis.

Elvis struck a pose, ran his hand through his pompadour and announced that the next song would close his show. He thrust the mic forward, leaned into it and cut loose with the leg-jiggling "Hound Dog." The audience responded with yells and claps that lasted well after the King slipped back behind the velvet curtain.

When we turned to leave the theater, Ed and Vic had vanished. Working our way through the throngs, we found them waiting for us in the car, where they sat fuming and scoffing like a couple of old high school jocks. Driving home, Merle and I mimicked Elvis singing "Hound Dog." We laughed so hard the guys couldn't help but join in.

What fun it had been to let down our hair and experience this teen idol in action. Merle and I remained avid Elvis fans long after he died in 1977. How sad that he's no longer with us. Now a white-haired grandmother, I'm unashamed to admit I still love Elvis Presley, the King forever!

BETTY J. VICKERS
ST. GEORGE, UT

Downtown Sycamore, left, in 1956 was home to Tony's, a popular hangout. At night, young people went to Teen Town, below, for the music.

Schooltime vs. Summertime

In youth, the year is divided into two seasons.

Growing up in Sycamore, Illinois, in the early 1950s was like growing up in Mayberry. The town's charm was as much a function of the times as it was the place. Although the Korean War was underway, those sights and sounds didn't invade our homes every night the way Vietnam did.

As teenagers, we had scant experience with class distinctions, racial injustice, unemployment or poverty. Maybe we were naive living in the American heartland, sheltered from the harsh realities of the world outside. Regardless, it was a wonderful time to be a teenager, and Sycamore was the best place to live.

As in most small towns, schools were the center of community activity. We respected our teachers and they cared about us. In those days, a call from the school to a parent about a child's behavior or bad grades was taken seriously.

To be expelled was the worst. Yet I recall one threatened expulsion that, in hindsight, seems unfair. John, a fine student and a solid citizen, was sent home for wearing sideburns. Remember, this was before Elvis or the Beatles were popular. John soon shaved his sideburns and returned to school.

Teen Town, Sycamore's recreation and social center, was established in 1953. Membership cost a nominal fee, and the center was open several nights a week. We went there to dance, play pingpong or hang out.

Few of us had jobs after school, but many young women I knew worked as carhops at the drive-in restaurants. The drive-in was another excuse to socialize, a place where boys and girls met, and romances bloomed.

During the summer, I detasseled corn for The Ag, the DeKalb Agricultural Association. The job lasted only a few weeks, but it was a quick way to make money for clothes and supplies for the upcoming school year. It also laid the foundation for my strong work ethic.

Summer was when I learned to play golf. If you lived in the Sycamore Park District, you could play rounds for free on Tuesday and Thursday mornings. After a few friends and I found some old golf clubs, we played there often.

If you or a parent worked for the Anaconda Wire and Cable Co., the park's outdoor pool was free, too. My sisters and I often hopped on our bicycles and rode there to swim for the entire afternoon.

The city's welcome sign once read: Life Offers More in Sycamore. It did in the '50s; maybe it's still true today.

GENE BEHLER · INDIANAPOLIS, IN

MAIN STREET, TEENS: COURTESY OF THE DEKALB COUNTY HISTORY CENTER

A LOOK BACK: UNIVERSAL PICTURES

Incorporated in 1912 as the Universal Film Manufacturing Co., it emerged as Hollywood's most celebrated movie studio, with a string of hits from such directors as Alfred Hitchcock and Steven Spielberg. Presented here are a few of Universal Pictures' most memorable films worth watching again in different genres.

MONSTERS

More than any other category, the monster movie is what made Universal Pictures famous. *The Phantom of the Opera* kicked things off in 1925—with actor Lon Chaney famously creating his own harrowing makeup. Then, in 1931, the one-two punch of Bela Lugosi's *Dracula* and Boris Karloff's *Frankenstein* secured the studio's reputation as Hollywood's house of horror.

1931
Dracula

1931
Frankenstein

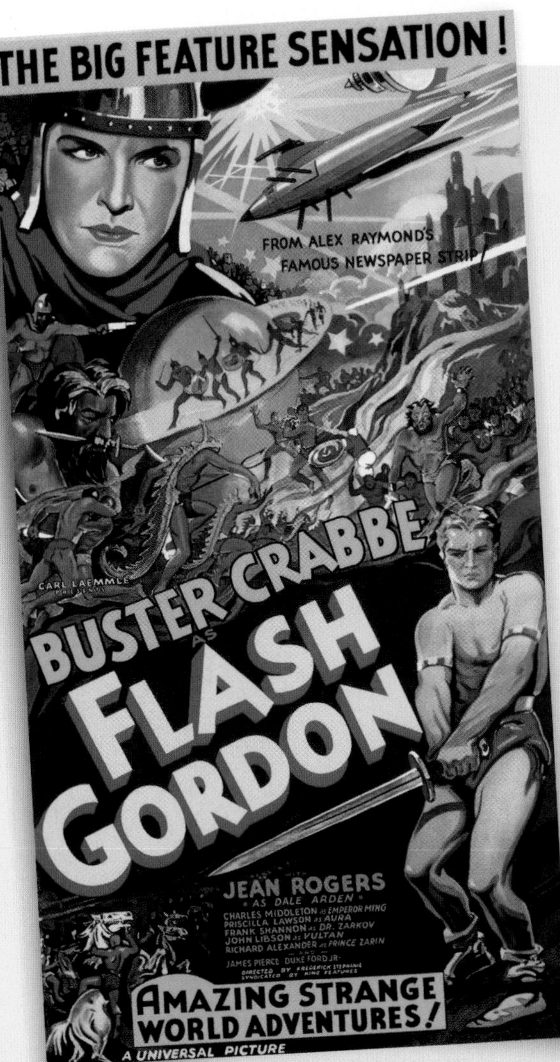

SCI-FI

Monster movies and science fiction go hand in hand, so it's no surprise that Universal had more than its share of otherworldly hits, including the special-effects-laden *It Came From Outer Space* in 1953 and *The Incredible Shrinking Man* in 1957. The studio also gave sci-fi fans their first big-screen *Flash Gordon*, delivering a 13-part serial in 1936. Based on the popular comic strip, debuting two years earlier, Universal's *Flash Gordon* starred Buster Crabbe.

1957
The Incredible Shrinking Man

1953
It Came From Outer Space

CLOCKWISE FROM FAR LEFT: SNAP/REX/SHUTTERSTOCK; TCD/PROD.DB/ALAMY STOCK PHOTO; PICTORIAL PRESS LTD/ALAMY STOCK PHOTO; AF ARCHIVE/ALAMY STOCK PHOTO (2); PICTURELUX/THE HOLLYWOOD ARCHIVE/ALAMY STOCK PHOTO

MUSICALS

If you need proof that Universal can carry a tune, look no further than Paul Robeson's epic rendition of "Ol' Man River" in *Show Boat*, the studio's 1936 film version of the stage musical by Jerome Kern and Oscar Hammerstein II. In 1967, it was Hollywood that inspired Broadway: The toe-tapping *Thoroughly Modern Millie*, starring Julie Andrews, led the way to a smash Broadway musical 35 years later.

1967
Thoroughly Modern Millie

1981
On Golden Pond

ROMANCE

Hopeless romantics have found plenty of reasons to love Universal Pictures over the years, from tear-jerkers like 1934's *Imitation of Life* and 1981's *On Golden Pond* to playful romantic romps like 1936's *My Man Godfrey* and 1979's *The Four Seasons*. But the studio's ultimate valentine to moviegoers proved to be the magical pairing of Rock Hudson and Doris Day. The duo appeared in 1959's *Pillow Talk*, 1961's *Lover Come Back* and 1964's *Send Me No Flowers*.

CLOCKWISE FROM FAR LEFT: PICTORIAL PRESS LTD/ALAMY STOCK PHOTO; ZUMA PRESS, INC./ALAMY STOCK PHOTO; MOVIESTORE

DRAMA

Not afraid to play it serious, Universal has produced some truly riveting dramas through the years, including 1932's gritty *Scarface*. The film adaptation of the novel *To Kill a Mockingbird* (1962) earned eight Academy Award nominations, and the American Film Institute named Gregory Peck's Atticus Finch the greatest movie hero of the 20th century.

1932
Scarface

1962
To Kill a Mockingbird

ACTION

War movies and Westerns are staples of the American cinema. And Universal has made a few of the best, including the gripping *All Quiet on the Western Front* (an Academy Award winner for best picture in 1930) and the enigmatic 1973 gunslinger picture *High Plains Drifter*, directed by and starring Clint Eastwood.

1973
High Plains Drifter

HITCHCOCK & SPIELBERG

No mention of Universal Pictures would be complete without a nod to the contributions of Alfred Hitchcock and Steven Spielberg—with *The Birds* and *Jaws* at the top of the list. In 1963, *The Birds* arrived as Hitchcock's follow-up to the masterful *Psycho*. Starring Rod Taylor and an unknown Tippi Hedren (in roles conceived for Cary Grant and Grace Kelly), it's a thriller that one critic called the director's "last unflawed film." And in 1975, up-and-comer Spielberg turned a problematic production—over budget and behind schedule—into what was then the highest-grossing movie ever: *Jaws* scared up $470 million at the box office.

1963
The Birds with Hitchcock and Tippi Hedren

LEGEND HAS IT COMPANY FOUNDER CARL LAEMMLE WAS INSPIRED TO USE THE UNIVERSAL NAME AFTER SEEING "UNIVERSAL PIPE FITTINGS" ON THE SIDE OF A PASSING DELIVERY TRUCK.

1933
Duck Soup

1950
Harvey

COMEDY

Universal had the Midas touch when it came to comedy. And the studio knew how to make the most of a good thing: 1947's *The Egg and I* introduced the characters of Ma and Pa Kettle, who rode out nine sequels together; in 1950, *Francis the Talking Mule* spawned six sequels. And Bud Abbott and Lou Costello made 36 movies together between 1940 and '56, many of them—including *Buck Privates* (1941) and *Abbott and Costello Meet Frankenstein* (1948)—for Universal.

Cinema Paradiso

Dad's movie theater was an inspiring place for a little girl to grow up.

Al Laurice loved the movie business. In this photo taken in 1953, Al is replacing the poster for the thriller *Angel Face* with one for the Academy Award-winning *From Here to Eternity*.

My father, Al Laurice, was 5 when he and his family left Ustica, Italy, and came to America in 1906. He worked in the movie industry all his life.

Dad got his start at the age of 20 with the Famous Players-Lasky Corp., which became Paramount Pictures. Then he took a sales and distribution job with 20th Century Fox, which took him to theaters throughout Northern California. He often took films to San Quentin State Prison for the inmates to enjoy, and I believe they appreciated his thoughtfulness.

When Dad took over the lease of the building that housed the Mayfield Theater in Palo Alto, he changed the name to the Cardinal. With the help of our family, he built a reputation for providing sophisticated entertainment to the Stanford University community. In the late '50s, the name of the business was changed to the Fine Arts Theater.

My three older siblings and I agreed that having a father in the theater business was exciting. Fred, Doug and Jo-Jean helped out in the theater, but I was too young to do much work. My memories are mostly of the fun I had: stretching out in the front row to watch movies, eating and drinking all the popcorn and cherry Coke I could consume, and accompanying Dad to the bus station to pick up films. I was a real daddy's girl and loved to spend time with him.

In 1954, when I was about 6, Dad won a lawsuit against Palo Alto's Advisory Board of Commercial Amusements, a group of citizens who reviewed films and rated them for content or banned them entirely. Encouraged by a '52 U.S. Supreme Court ruling that the First Amendment protected motion pictures, he argued that the board made it hard for him to compete with movie theaters in nearby Menlo Park, which had no such civic censors. Dad's good friend Robert Winslow helped with the case. Palo Alto's board was soon abolished.

I remember Dad as a quiet, mellow guy, so I was surprised to learn years later that he had stood up to censorship. He passed away when I was 14, and I miss him to this day.

WENDY HORTON
ROHNERT PARK, CA

The Magic Lives On

The Wizard of Oz inspired many terrific vintage novelties. Check out these antiques from 1939-1940.

BY JAY SCARFONE AND WILLIAM STILLMAN

JUDY GARLAND AS DOROTHY DOLL
Ideal Novelty & Toy Co.—makers of the wildly popular Shirley Temple doll of the same era—offered the Judy Garland doll in three sizes. The largest, at 18 inches (shown here), sold for $5.

BOARD GAME
Whitman Publishing Co. released this item with characters that were hybrids of their depictions in the *Oz* books and the film. It originally sold for 25 cents.

PAPER MASKS
Einson-Freeman Co. issued a set of five paper masks of the *Oz* movie characters. The set featured Dorothy, the Scarecrow, the Tin Man, the Cowardly Lion and the Wizard, accompanied by a flyer titled "Eight Ways to Have Fun at a Hallowe'en Party With *Wizard of Oz* Masks."

THEMED SCARVES
Brian Fabrics sold rayon *Wizard of Oz* scarves in two designs and a variety of colors.

FLYING MONKEYS IN COLOR, OH MY!

I WASN'T QUITE 8 years old when *The Wizard of Oz* debuted, but I was especially interested in seeing it because my name is Dorothy. After all the advertising and hoopla, Mom finally took my brother and me to see the movie.

Most films at that time were in black and white, so the audience was spellbound when Dorothy's house landed in Oz and everything turned into glorious Technicolor. Needless to say, everyone enjoyed the movie—except me. The flying monkeys frightened me and made me hide my head! To this day, after 75 years and many more viewings with my children and grandchildren, I still view the monkeys with apprehension.

About the time the movie opened, I attended a one-room school where all eight grades were taught. Mom bought me an *Oz* picture book, which I took to class to show my teacher. Miss Freehling had me stand in front of the whole school to read the story. I was so nervous!

DOROTHY BRNIK • HUMMELSTOWN, PA

Winged monkeys spooked young Dorothy Brnik (above) more than the Wicked Witch when she first saw the movie.

10 THINGS YOU DIDN'T KNOW ABOUT *OZ*

There certainly is something special about The Wizard of Oz *that has kept fans captivated for decades.*

BY JAY SCARFONE AND WILLIAM STILLMAN

1

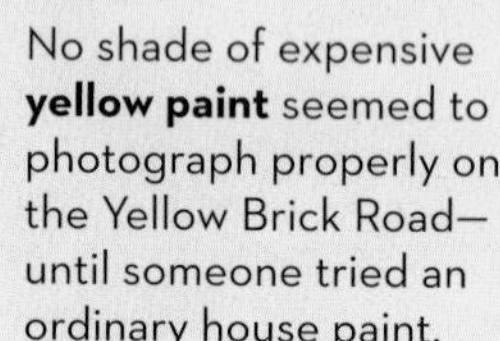

No shade of expensive **yellow paint** seemed to photograph properly on the Yellow Brick Road—until someone tried an ordinary house paint.

2

Judy Garland was 16 years old when filming began. California law permitted her, as a minor, to work only four hours a day.

3

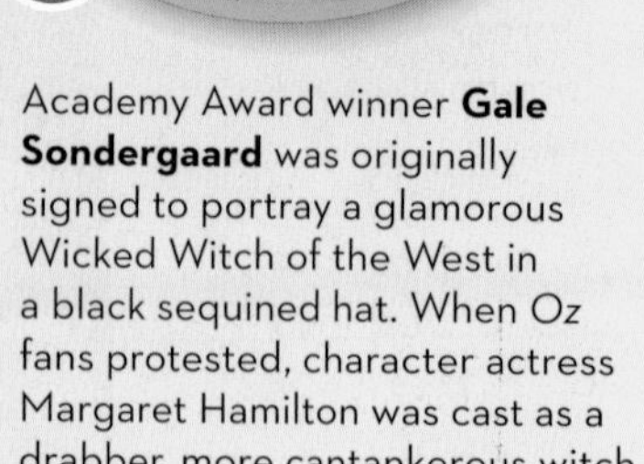

Academy Award winner **Gale Sondergaard** was originally signed to portray a glamorous Wicked Witch of the West in a black sequined hat. When Oz fans protested, character actress Margaret Hamilton was cast as a drabber, more cantankerous witch.

4

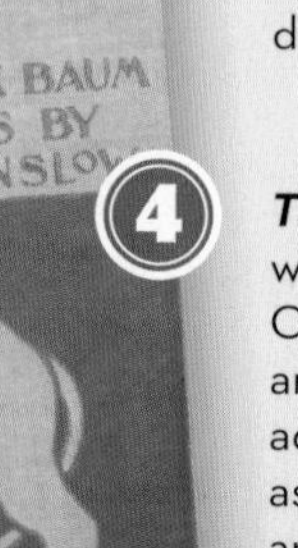

The Wonderful Wizard of Oz wasn't Dorothy's only journey to Oz! L. Frank Baum wrote 14 novels and six short stories about her adventures. Recent movies such as *Oz, The Great and Powerful* and *Dorothy of Oz* were based on these books. The Bradford Press has re-created these elaborately illustrated first editions.

5

The jacket **Frank Morgan** wore as Professor Marvel came from a thrift shop. MGM spread the story that, by coincidence, the jacket was later found to have belonged to L. Frank Baum.

The **winged monkeys** soared through the air with the aid of piano wire.

There are no characters representing Miss Gulch or Professor Marvel in Baum's book—the screenwriters created these parts. The movie version also merges two good witches into a single character: **Glinda, the Good Witch of the North**.

The 1939 movie is a remake. Two **silent film versions** preceded it, in 1910 and 1925. The latter starred Oliver Hardy as the character then called simply the Woodsman.

Ray Bolger wore an asbestos version of his Scarecrow costume for the scene in which the Wicked Witch lights him on fire. Men with fire extinguishers stood out of camera range.

When it was released in 1939, *The Wizard of Oz* rarely played in theaters more than three nights. Though it became a top moneymaker that year, *Oz* didn't recoup its **$3 million production costs** until its rerelease 10 years later.

SCARFONE/STILLMAN COLLECTION (10)

Going to See the 'Picture Show'

Enjoying movies in his small town in the 1950s was a sinful treat.

fter the difficulties of the Great Depression and World War II and before the crazy world of adulthood was the slower, laid-back time when I was a boy of the 1950s. One of the joys of that special time for kids was going to the movies.

Back then we called it the "picture show," not the movies. To us, anything on the big screen was fantastic. We'd go see shows we really weren't that interested in just for the experience. And, of course, the popcorn.

My hometown of Bristow, Oklahoma, had two indoor theaters, the Princess and the Walmur. We attended the Walmur most often because the 15-cent admission was a dime cheaper than the other.

My best buddy, Richard, and I got jobs delivering show calendars once a month for the Princess. We had been delivering the Tulsa newspapers for several years, so we knew the layout of our small town. Mr. Simpson, the theater's owner and operator, paid us each 75 cents plus five free movie passes. That was quite a lot for a teenager in the '50s.

Richard and I would go straight to Dairy Queen to celebrate our newly acquired wealth with huge 10-cent dip ice cream cones.

The downside of going to shows back then was that it was listed as a sin by certain churches, mine included. I couldn't see why God didn't want me to see a great movie. So I decided that the sin designation had to be a mistake made by some old deacons who didn't like movies or who didn't want kids to have fun.

Oh sure, my young conscience still bothered me enough so I'd never linger at the ticket window, which was highly visible from Main Street. I could purchase a ticket and be inside in record time. If the ticket line had more than two or three people in it, I'd amble down the sidewalk and look in the

The Princess Theatre was one of two movie houses in Bristow, Oklahoma, providing endless fascination for Nick Aston and other boys like him.

Western Auto window to kill time before I dashed back to make my purchase.

That guilt didn't help when walking home after a rather scary movie. I'd walk quickly down the middle of the street so nothing evil could reach out and grab me. One night, upon seeing a large dark figure near one of the houses, I decided it was best to speak. I said hello very quickly and picked up my already brisk pace. The next day I realized I'd spoken to a cedar tree!

Being young and uninformed on upcoming feature movies, I saw an ad that quickly got my attention. *Giant* was playing at the Purple Pirate Drive-In west of town. I hitched a ride like we did a lot back then, looking forward to seeing a movie about dinosaurs or monsters. I was pretty disappointed to find out that the movie was about discovering oil in Texas.

I hold close these fond memories of going to the picture show—long before megaplex theaters and a $20 tab for a ticket, a Coke and some popcorn. Thank goodness the popcorn smells just as good.

NICK ASTON • JENKS, OK

WEDDING NIGHT AT THE FOX

She had a starring role when *Father of the Bride* came to town.

I WORKED AT THE FOX THEATRE in Hutchinson, Kansas, and enjoyed some memorable promotions, including my night as a stand-in for Elizabeth Taylor.

When the Fox opened in 1931, it was a big deal. The *Hutchinson News* called it "one of the finest theaters it is possible to build." The theater marquee was said to be the state's first display of flashing neon lights in Kansas. (It still works today and is a colorful part of the restored theater.) A special bonus was "refrigeration," the term used back then for air conditioning.

The theater also had live midnight music shows after the movies, bringing in Xavier Cugat, Les Brown and His Band of Renown, and other big names.

I worked at the Fox 30 hours a week at 40 cents an hour in my last two years of high school. That $12 went a long way toward school needs and spending money.

Employees would wear cowboy and cowgirl outfits when a Western was coming to town, and there'd even be horses outside the theater. In those days, moviegoing was truly magical.

My best memory of working at the theater is from the summer of 1950, when I wore a copy of Elizabeth Taylor's wedding dress from the movie *Father of the Bride*.

The dress was on display for a couple of weeks before the movie came to town. Then, on July 29, the night of the first showing at the Fox, the C.O. Mammel Bakery in Hutchinson contributed a wedding cake. And I was the lucky one who got to wear that fancy dress and serve up pieces of cake to celebrate the premiere!

JOAN NELSON • WICHITA, KS

JUNGLE LOVE

Edgar Rice Burroughs introduced his lord of the apes in *The All-Story* magazine. Former Olympic swimmer Johnny Weissmuller hit the big screen later as Tarzan in 12 motion pictures—six with MGM and six more with RKO.

1932

Tarzan, The Ape Man; MGM; with Maureen O'Sullivan as Jane and Neil Hamilton as Harry Holt

1941

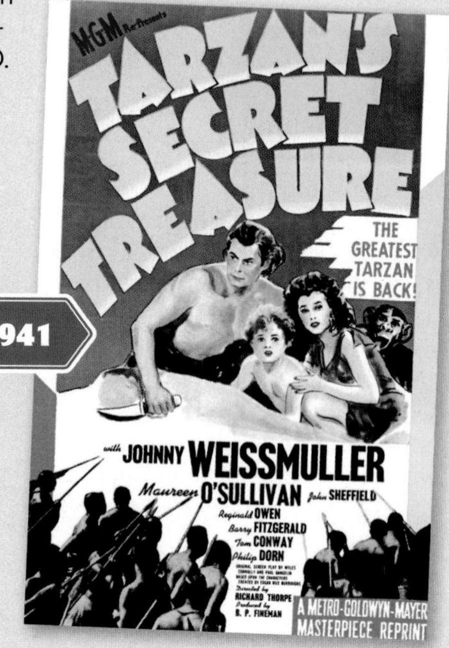

Tarzan's Secret Treasure; MGM; with Maureen O'Sullivan as Jane, John Sheffield as Boy

Tarzan Finds a Son; MGM; with Maureen O'Sullivan as Jane, John Sheffield as Boy

1939

PHOTOS 12/ALAMY STOCK PHOTO (6); *TARZAN AND THE HUNTRESS*: RKO/KOBAL/SHUTTERSTOCK

1943

Tarzan Triumphs; RKO; with Johnny Sheffield as Boy and Frances Gifford as Zandra

1947

Tarzan and the Huntress; RKO; with Brenda Joyce as Jane and Johnny Sheffield as Boy

1946

Tarzan and the Leopard Woman; RKO; with Brenda Joyce as Jane and Johnny Sheffield as Boy

Tarzan and the Mermaids; RKO; with Brenda Joyce as Jane

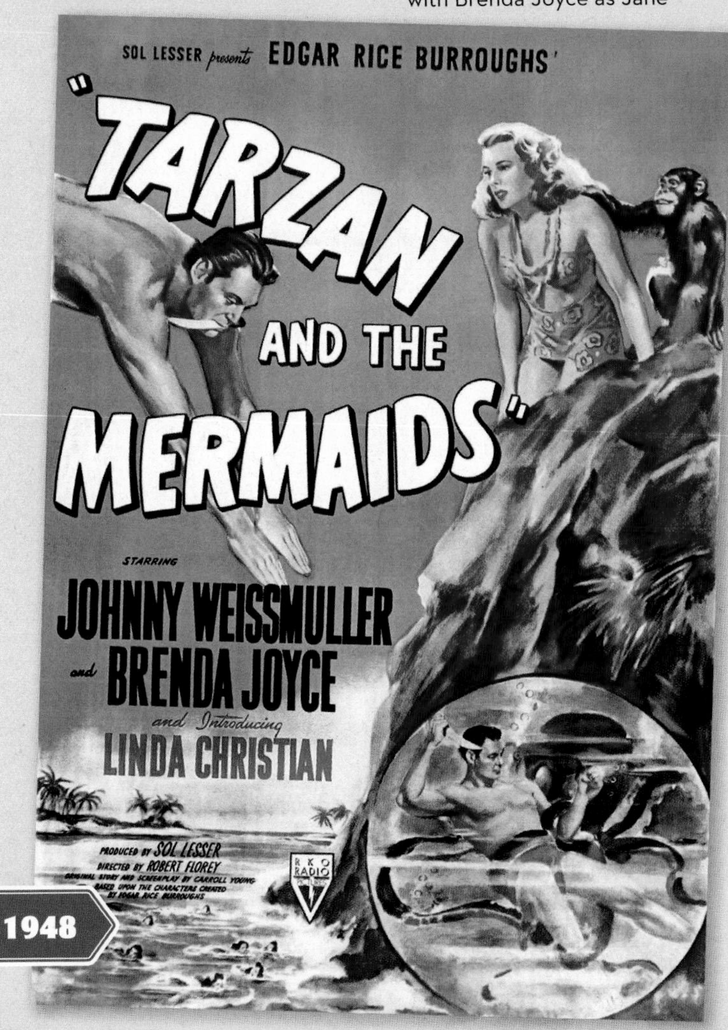

1948

THE WORLD ON SCREEN

From theater to living room, entertainment shifted as TVs, projectors and more became readily available. Life got better when it could be watched at home.

1947

The Revere Camera Co. glorified the growing home movie craze of the late '40s with a line of 8 mm cameras and supporting devices, such as a splicer for editing.

1978

This Zenith ad, which ran in *Time*, came a mere three years after Sony introduced the VCR to the world. By 1984, one in seven U.S. households would own a VCR.

1962

A stunning Motorola ad features electronics in ultracontemporary settings. Here, architect Leon Deller's subterranean rec room design has aquarium windows that look into the backyard pool. Notice the TV remote to the man's left.

TYPICAL SOAP DAY

11 A.M.
Watch *The Young and the Restless* and see Victor Newman fall in love with a younger woman.

11:10 A.M.
The Tide commercial reminds me to put in a load of laundry.

11:30 A.M.
See glamorous Laurie's lioness hairdo. Love it!

11:45 A.M.
During the commercial, write a note to buy shampoo to make my hair look like Laurie's.

NOON
Tune to *All My Children*. What is scheming Erica Kane up to?

12:15 P.M.
Put the laundry into dryer during the ads.

12:30 P.M.
Listen to Tad Martin argue with parents Ruth and Joe.

12:45 P.M.
Set up ironing board and lay out pork chops to thaw.

1 P.M.
Yay! *One Life to Live* is on!

1:10 P.M.
Sprinkle Comet into the sink when a commercial comes on for the product. Go back to TV.

1:15 P.M.
Observe calculating Tina get into mischief.

1:30 P.M.
Go get the mail.

1:45 P.M.
Listen to Viki and Clint's marital problems.

2 P.M.
It's time for *General Hospital*. Watch Dr. Hardy console Jessie, the kind nurse.

2:15 P.M.
Dust the coffee table and the end tables.

2:30 P.M.
See Luke and Laura get married.

2:45 P.M.
Vacuum the hallway.

CATHY WILSON
BUHL, ID

In the '80s, when I was in high school, I would head off campus at lunchtime to the Kmart store next door. Once there, I'd head to the back, where the televisions were. I'd find a cozy seat, unpack my lunch and watch *As the World Turns*.

MARIA RUPERT • GALESBURG, IL

HER SOAP NAME

Dawn is my middle name, and that's what everyone in my family has always called me, except my father. Dad called me by my given name, Julie. That's because I was named after his favorite character from *Days of Our Lives*. I'm glad he called me Julie. It was a special something just between us. By the way, that's me sitting on my mother's lap.

JULIE DAWN NIX • TOCCOA, GA

GENERAL HOSPITAL: PICTURELUX/THE HOLLYWOOD ARCHIVE/ALAMY STOCK PHOTO

Edward G. Robinson and Sammy Davis Jr. were among the celebrities who popped up in batclimbs. By the last season, the gag was wearing thin, with dubious "stars" like Los Angeles' TV carpet king Cyril Lord, shown here.

BURST: JO RITCHY/SHUTTERSTOCK; BATCLIMB: ZUMA PRESS INC./ALAMY STOCK PHOTO; ROBIN: AF ARCHIVE/ALAMY STOCK PHOTO; VILLAINS: PHOTOS 12/ALAMY STOCK PHOTO

A VERITABLE VILLAGE OF VILLAINY

THE CHANCE TO OVERACT with evil glee had an array of widely known character actors and A-list stars, including Oscar winners, clamoring to join the show's gallery of rogues. Most *Batman* villains appeared in only one episode or story line, but a few were so good that producers brought them back to chew up the scenery again and again.

THE JOKER
Cesar Romero, 22 episodes

THE PENGUIN
Burgess Meredith, 21 episodes

CATWOMAN
Julie Newmar, 13 episodes
Eartha Kitt, 5 episodes

THE RIDDLER
Frank Gorshin, 10 episodes
John Astin, 2 episodes

KING TUT
Victor Buono, 10 episodes

EGGHEAD
Vincent Price, 7 episodes

LOUIE THE LILAC
Milton Berle, 5 episodes

CHANDELL/HARRY
Liberace, 2 episodes

MR. FREEZE
George Sanders, Otto Preminger, Eli Wallach, 2 episodes each

MA PARKER
Shelley Winters, 2 episodes

Batman's most oppressive opponents formed the United Underworld in *Batman: The Movie*. Lee Meriwether played Catwoman in the film.

ROBIN'S SACRED OATHS

THE BOY WONDER may not have had Batman's fancy gadgets, but he did have a way with words. His "holy" phrases—more than 350 of them—reveal a surprising range of knowledge, from the scientific (Holy Reverse Polarity) to the political (Holy Fourth Amendment) to the literary (Holy Hamlet). Here are a few more favorites:

Holy Knit One, Purl Two

Holy Contributing to the Delinquency of Minors

Holy Astringent Plumlike Fruit

Holy Uncanny Photographic Mental Processes

Holy Hole in a Doughnut

Holy Floor Covering

Holy Impregnability

Holy Human Surfboards

Holy Benedict Arnold

Holy Return from Oblivion

Holy Subliminal

Holy Priceless Collection of Etruscan Snoods

Holy Non Sequiturs

Holy Wayne Manor

Holy Cliché

Sir Alfred Hitchcock's ability to scare us got him a knighthood.

TERROR IN THE BEDROOM

THERE WAS AN EPISODE of *Alfred Hitchcock Presents* about a nurse named Stella who had taken part in burying someone in a cellar wall. I was so frightened, I couldn't fall asleep that night. There I was in my bed, lights off and eyes wide open. And then I heard it: a soft voice murmuring, "Stella, Stella..." It was my brother, hiding under my bed, trying to scare me! Needless to say, he succeeded.

ANTONETTE NONNI • CAMBRIDGE, MA

PARDON ME, MS. MANNEQUIN

ROD SERLING'S *The Twilight Zone* was not to be missed. Even though I was a kid, the eerie happenings made my hair stand on end. I'll never forget one episode in particular. Set in a department store, it revolved around a woman played by Anne Francis. The elevator let her off on the fifth floor, which was not open to the public. Stored up there were all the mannequins—who just so happened to come alive. Turns out, she was a mannequin also! To this day, I am always respectful of mannequins and say "Excuse me" if I bump into one. You just can't take any chances.

TONI SPARKS • COLORADO SPRINGS, CO

Rod Serling, who created *The Twilight Zone* and *Night Gallery*, wrote the movie *Planet of the Apes*.

TV: AFRICA STUDIO/SHUTTERSTOCK; HITCHCOCK, SERLING, DE CARLO: PICTURELUX/THE HOLLYWOOD ARCHIVE/ALAMY STOCK PHOTO; FRID: RGR COLLECTION/ALAMY STOCK PHOTO

If Barnabas Collins (Jonathan Frid) didn't scare you, what would?

FANGS FOR THE MEMORIES

WHEN I WAS GROWING UP, my bedroom walls were covered with photos from *Dark Shadows*, the Gothic soap opera that ran every weekday from 1966 to 1971. My favorite was a glow-in-the-dark poster of the vampire Barnabas Collins baring his fangs. Once, my mother paid me $300 to take it down while a relative was visiting.

JANYTH THOMPSON • BRANCHLAND, WV

HANGING WITH LILY MUNSTER

IT HAPPENED IN Bakersfield, California, in 1987: I stopped at a motel bar to have a drink and started talking to a dark-haired lady. We even danced to the country band playing. Then it struck me—she resembled a famous movie star. I started to tell her, but she abruptly cut me off: "Don't say it. I am who you think I am."

It was Yvonne De Carlo. I could not believe it! I even had a crush on a girl in high school just because she reminded me of her.

BARRY DAVID KIBLER • PARADISE, CA

In addition to *The Munsters*, Yvonne De Carlo starred in *The Ten Commandments*.

ONE STEP TOO MANY

ONE STEP BEYOND, hosted by John Newland, ran from 1959 to 1961. These were supposed to be true stories, which set the show apart from others of its ilk. In one episode, a young married couple had an argument on their front porch, and the wife stormed into the house. When her husband went in after her, she was gone, never to be heard from again. Since I was only 12, I had the idea this could happen to me, so for years, I refused to go into the house alone.

SHEILA HURTEAU • ORLEANS, MA

Frustrated for $200, Alex

The real trick to succeeding at *Jeopardy!* was not just knowing the answer, but knowing how to play the buzzer.

My children suggested I try out for *Jeopardy!* I was a college teacher and lived in Calabasas, California, close to Los Angeles, so I thought, why not?

These days you take the test online, but in 1990 you had to call the local TV station affiliate to register. There were about 100 people waiting at the test site. They gave each of us a sheet of paper with space for 100 answers, and they warned us that the questions would come very quickly and cover a variety of topics. You had to answer fast and there was no time to go back if you missed one. About 15 of us made it through that first round.

Next, they divided us into groups of three. They stood us in front of a TV monitor, a school bell in front of each contestant. It was a simulated show, with questions coming up on the monitor. If you knew the answer, you rang the bell as soon as possible. Then they took a photo of each of us and told us to wait for a callback.

A week or so later, I got my call. My appearance was with two other women, one of them a returning champion.

The real trick to succeeding at *Jeopardy!* was not just knowing the answer (or "question," in *Jeopardy!* parlance), but also knowing how to play the buzzer. Press it too early and you'd be blocked out, too late and you'd be beaten. The champions have an edge because they've had more practice with the darn buzzer. (Several years later, *Jeopardy!* changed its policy, giving all new contestants a few practice rounds with the buzzer to even their chances.)

I came in second with a score of $12,000, and I got the Final Jeopardy question—"Who is Oprah Winfrey?" After the show aired, friends would hum the *Jeopardy!* theme song whenever I walked into a room.

BARBARA PIXLEY • FREDERICKSBURG, VA

Jeopardy! host Alex Trebek has won six Daytime Emmys during his time on the show, and in 2013 he was inducted into the Broadcasting & Cable Hall of Fame.

LEFT: COURTESY EVERETT COLLECTION

LOYAL LISTENER

My father took this 1949 slide of me listening to the radio at our home in Grand Ledge, Michigan. Apparently the radio on the bottom didn't get all the stations we liked, so we sat another one on top of it to make sure we didn't miss those great programs. I always liked the radio shows and still enjoy them on satellite radio.

DOUG SCHLAPPI • SUNFIELD, MI

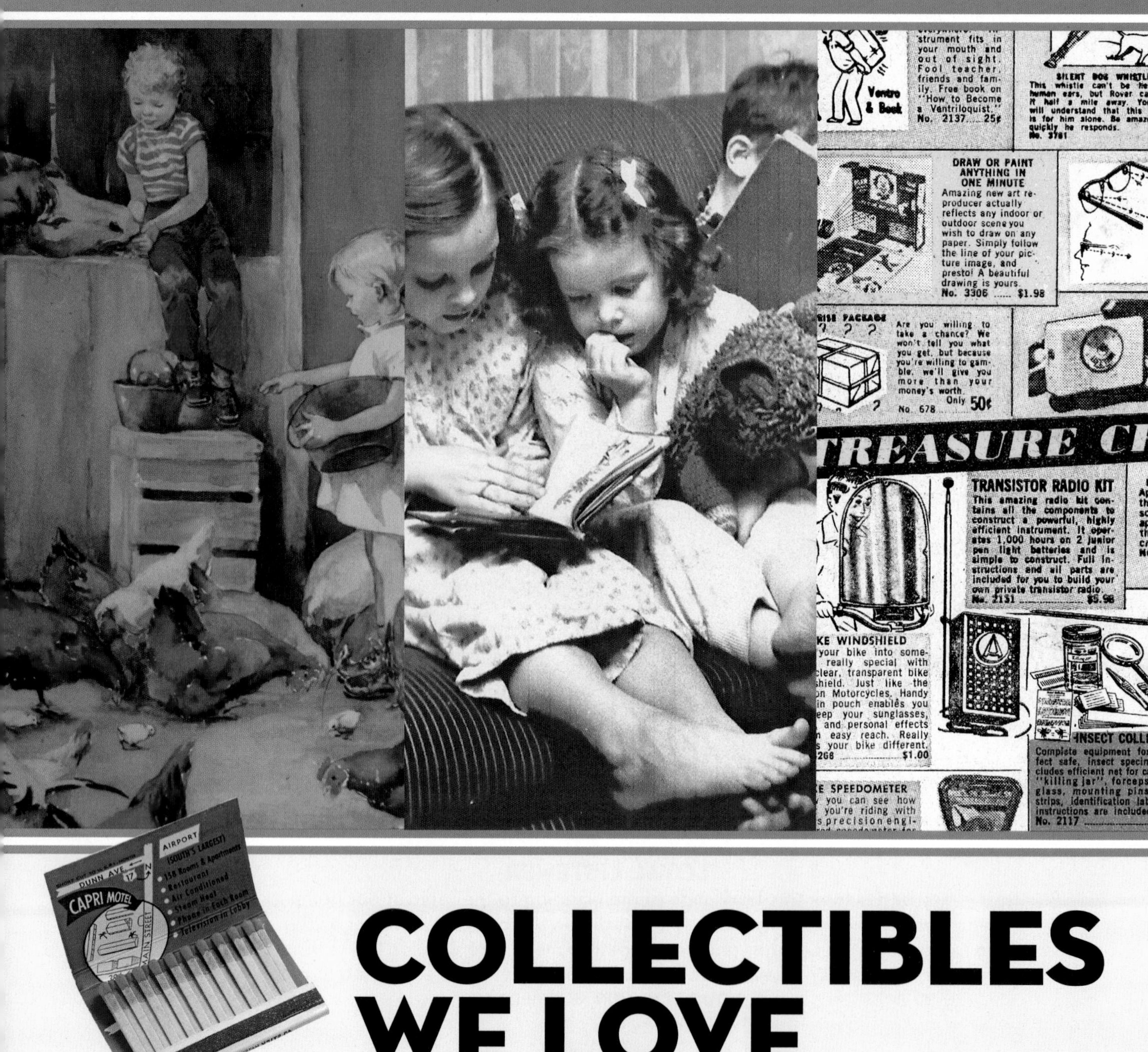

COLLECTIBLES WE LOVE

CHAPTER 6

Stumbling upon items from days long gone gives us a sense of nostalgia that sometimes nothing else can. And the satisfaction of completing a collection or the joy in finding the perfect treasure is priceless.

A Striking History

More than 100 years ago, the world's smallest billboards set the advertising world on fire.

BY KEN WYSOCKY

From television and radio commercials to Twitter and Facebook and everything else in between, advertising has come a long way in the last century. But amid today's endless blitz of sophisticated marketing methods, it's easy to forget that for decades, the country's most popular advertising medium was matchbooks, which fit in the palm of one's hand as easily as a smartphone and got the message across in a way that was succinct, graphic and mobile.

From gas stations and restaurants to tourist attractions and political campaigns, matchbooks were the way to get the word out. Super easy to distribute and ridiculously inexpensive (about $5 for a case of 2,500 matchbooks in the 1920s) they quickly became a hot marketing medium.

Any phillumenist—someone who collects matchbooks and related memorabilia—can tell you that a Philadelphia lawyer, Joshua Pusey, invented the matchbook around 1890. A few years later he sold the patent rights to the Diamond Match Co., which proceeded to dominate the American market for decades.

It's commonly believed that in 1895, a traveling opera company became one of the first groups to use matchbooks for commercial advertising. Members hand-decorated blank matchbooks to promote an opening night performance, which reportedly led to a sold-out house.

That glowing ember of an idea became a roaring bonfire in 1902, when Milwaukee's Pabst Brewing Co. placed an order with Diamond for an astounding 10 million matchbooks to advertise its Pabst Blue Ribbon beer.

Not to be outdone, Chicago's William Wrigley Jr. Co. soon followed with an even more astonishing amount: 1 billion matchbooks advertising their chewing gum.

Safety enhancements—such as placing the match striker on the outside of the matchbook and adding the ubiquitous warning, "Close Cover Before Striking"—and the increasing popularity of cigarettes

Continued on page 162 ▸

PREVIOUS SPREAD: SUPERMAN: HULTON ARCHIVE/GETTY IMAGES; ALL MATCHBOOKS THIS SPREAD AND NEXT: H. VINCENT PEFFLEY

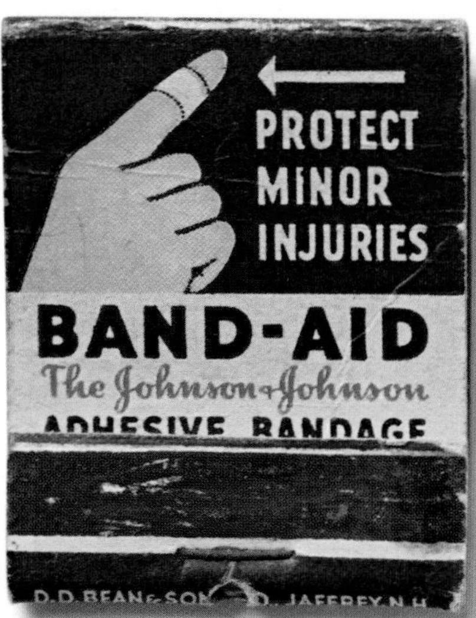

Matchbooks warmed advertisers' hearts with their ability to keep company names top-of-mind for less than a penny each.

COMBUSTIBLE COLLECTIBLES

When I was about 9 years old in Goshen, Indiana, I started to collect matchbooks. Collecting things like stamps and baseball cards was big in the early 1940s; most boys needed to keep busy when they weren't playing baseball.

Having been a Depression baby, I was taught to watch my pennies. That's why I began collecting matchbooks: You could pick them up just about anywhere for free.

When my Aunt Sally learned about my hobby, she gave me a matchbook album in which to store them, along with many matchbook covers from New York City. That really got me going.

Early on, most of my haul carried advertisements for local businesses and political candidates. But as my horizons broadened with age, so did my collection—and my enthusiasm for it.

My collecting slowed down during my busy years in high school, the U.S. Navy and college, and while raising a family. But after our children grew up, my wife, Nancy, and I started to travel more, which rekindled my interest.

I now have about 1,500 matchbooks stored in albums, old tobacco cans and shoe and cigar boxes. They're like souvenirs of all the hotels, motels, restaurants and tourist attractions we've visited over the years—and they take up less space than most souvenirs.

I've donated 235 matchbooks to the Goshen Historical Society. Most of them carry ads for businesses in northern Indiana, as well as for political campaigns. They're on display and provide interesting glimpses into the area's history—all thanks to that simple, inexpensive hobby I started many years ago.

H. VINCENT PEFFLEY
OTTAWA, ILLINOIS

boosted their prevalence. By the 1920s, colorful printed matchbooks became one of the country's most prolific kinds of advertising.

But the fortunes of matchbook advertising flickered somewhat briefly during the Great Depression. Diamond rekindled the flame by producing collectible sets adorned with photos of movie stars like George Raft and Katharine Hepburn. The move was so popular that other collectible sets followed, featuring professional and college sports personalities.

In 1945, aided by patriotic wartime ads, the industry produced more than 500 billion matches, including 200 billion that were nestled inside matchbooks. It's easy to understand their popularity: At a cost of about one-fifth of a cent each, matchbooks remained an easily affordable advertising method for many.

Boosted by postwar economic growth, sales of matchbooks peaked in the 1950s. Nowadays, collectors prize these miniature works of art, which cleverly reflect the artistic, business and cultural tenor of their times.

And at an amazingly low cost of about 2 cents per matchbook, these little cultural touchstones still remain an inexpensive, low-tech and effective advertising staple for countless numbers of small businesses—no internet connection required.

Just about anything—from flying lessons to water-skiing shows—was fair game for the outside or inside of a matchbook. Many phillumenists enjoy collecting matchbooks because these small time capsules vividly reflect the sensibilities of their eras. H. Vincent Peffley collected matchbooks as a boy growing up in Indiana. Eventually, he amassed over 1,500 of them. The matchbooks pictured on these pages come from his collection.

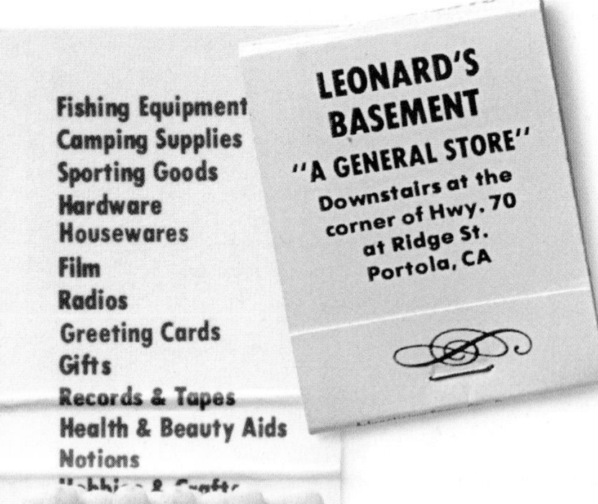

BEAUTIFUL ARRANGEMENTS

Reasonably priced flower frogs leap into today's home decor.

BY JOE KENZ AND SANDY GARRISON

FLOWER HOLDERS known as frogs have become popular collectibles thanks to their whimsical appearance, variety and relative availability. It's not clear how the term "frog" came to be associated with this item; it may simply have been a piece of slang that stuck. Makes sense, though: The holders, when they are full of flower stems and submerged in shallow water, resemble their amphibious namesakes.

1 SCARF DANCER FLOWER FROG

Most likely produced in Czechoslovakia or Germany sometime between 1920 and World War II, this flower frog is shaped like a scarf dancer, a popular motif at the time. Though this frog has no markings, it was likely made for Ebeling & Reuss Co., a large importer of giftware that operated in Pennsylvania from 1900 to 2002. Some Ebeling & Reuss frogs are marked "Erphila," a combination of the founder's initials and Philadelphia. Glazes on these frogs vary from snow white to ivory, although some have colors. Cracking or crazing in the glaze is very common and can cause the piece to discolor with age.

2 GLASS FLOWER FROG

By the beginning of the 20th century, many United States companies were producing glass frogs. As a result, they are plentiful today. Most are not marked, although frogs made by Ohio's A.H. Heisey and Co. Inc. and the Cambridge Glass Co. are exceptions. They also can be repurposed as pencil holders or lovely paperweights.

3 BLUE RIBBON FLOWER HOLDER

Ohio's Ida Sinclair became well-known around Cuyahoga Falls for her award-winning flower arrangements, and one of her secrets turned out to be a homemade frog, crafted from strategically bent bobby pins stuck into a circular lead base. The idea became so popular, Ida patented it in 1936 and opened her own business, which still produces the holders in much the same way.

4 REYNOLDS FLORAL ARRANGER

With its rearrangeable metal arms, this 1950s-era frog offered users the flexibility that made cage frogs popular—a variety of stem sizes could be used in many different configurations, as explained in an accompanying instruction booklet.

FLOWER FROGS 2, 3 AND 4: SANDY GARRISON

COLLECTOR'S CORNER

Souvenirs From the Past

Collectibles of the 1893 Chicago world's fair provide a glimpse into another time.

BY JOE KENZ AND SANDY GARRISON

Showcasing ingenuity and achievement are goals of all world's fairs, but the 1893 World's Columbian Exposition, also known as the Chicago world's fair, set the benchmark for those that followed. Souvenirs from the event capture a bit of that magic and are popular with collectors today.

① POSTCARD

While postcards started circulating in Europe around 1870, early examples were intended as commemoratives or used for advertising. The cards produced for the fair were the first to be sold as souvenirs, and they are plentiful. At the time, the post office didn't allow any correspondence on the address side, so message space was left on the front.

② COLUMBUS EGG PUZZLE

Produced by Chicago's P.M. Baumgardner & Co., this nickel-plated egg has two counterweights inside. The puzzle is to align the weights so that the egg balances on its point. It was made in reference to an account of Christopher Columbus getting a real egg to stand vertically, and was patented just as the exposition was beginning.

③ LIBBEY GLASS

Edward Libbey decided to exhibit his struggling glassware company at the Columbian Exposition, despite opposition from the company's board. The risk paid off. More than 2 million people visited the display, turning Libbey Glass into a household name. The pavilion charged admission and featured a working glass factory—and offered a wide range of souvenirs, including a variety of paperweights.

④ DECK OF PLAYING CARDS

These decorated decks typically feature fair scenes and historical personalities. Single cards will sell, but complete decks in their original boxes have the highest value. The set pictured here was manufactured by the World's Fair Souvenir Card Co., designed and lithographed by the Winters Art Lithographing Co.

5 HEINZ PICKLE
Concerned that fairgoers wouldn't climb the stairs to visit his second-floor exhibit, H.J. Heinz distributed printed tags promising a free gift. Visitors who mounted the steps received a pickle-shaped charm made of the natural latex gutta-percha. "Heinz's Keystone" was marked on the charm. H.J. Heinz's plan was so successful that the floor sagged from the amount of traffic it caused. A later version of the charm, made of plastic, is still available.

GOOD SIGNS

Vintage farm placards add instant charm and a rustic vibe. Find one that speaks to you.

BY JOE KENZ

GOOSE BREEDER & POTATOES AND ONIONS

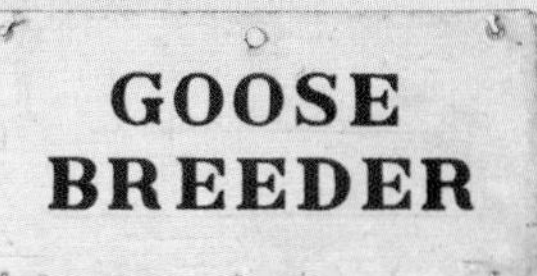

Often produced on the farm by a talented family member, some hand-painted signs are considered on a level with folk art. The value depends on the subject, complexity, color and condition, and images or designs can add significant value. Both examples pictured here date to about 1950 and are painted on wooden boards, "potatoes" in freehand script and the other using stencils.

PRIDE SEED DEALER

Branded seed-dealer signs are numerous, with collectors of certain companies as loyal as sports fans. Pride produces seed for Canadian farmers. This sign is a die-cut metal example dating to circa 1960; it was modified to include the dealer's name.

PURINA CHOWS

Founded in 1894, Ralston Purina became one of the largest suppliers of animal feed in the industry, and its iconic red-and-white checkerboard logo is easily recognized. This metal sign, featuring the name of the farmer, was probably given as a promotional item in the 1940s. The rust and scratched paint diminish its value.

CHESTER'S COMPLETE FARM SERVICE

Orville Redenbacher (of popcorn fame) and his partner, Charles Bowman, purchased the George F. Chester & Sons Seed Co. in 1947 and established Chester Inc. The company continues to offer a wide variety of agricultural services, from seeds to technology support to building project advice. The image on this 1950s sign, despite some wear, increases its winsome appeal.

JOHN DEERE

The John Deere brand is popular with collectors. This near-mint, partially embossed 1930s dealer sign hung in an Indiana hardware store with the dealer's name in the "privilege panel."

WORLD'S FAIR COLLECTIBLES AND SIGNS: SANDY GARRISON

Old School

Vintage globes, desks and crayon boxes go from classroom necessities to home collectibles.

BY JOE KENZ

SCHOOL SUPPLIES

Pencil, crayon and paint boxes from manufacturers such as Dixon, Binney & Smith and Faber-Castell often feature great graphics, making them fun to display on a desk or in a library. These examples date from 1930-1960.

EDUCATIONAL GAMES

Valued today for their colorful illustrations, instructional games were used to teach words, numbers and more. Companies such as Milton Bradley, Parker Brothers and A.I. Root produced anagrams like these about 1930-1960.

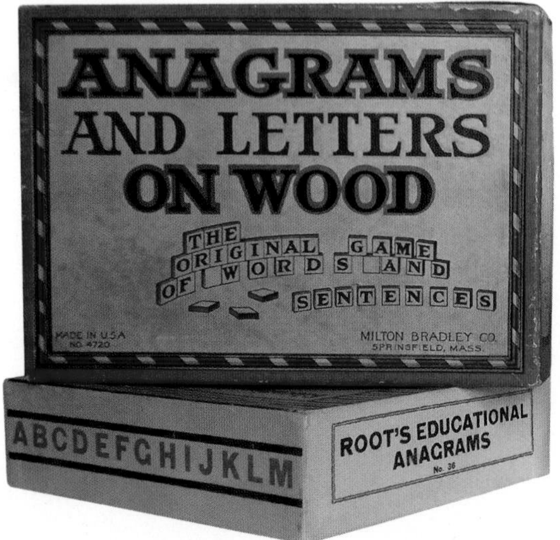

GLOBE

Retro globes add color and simple charm to any room of the home. Chicago-area company Rand McNally sold this one in the 1970s. Older models are often worth more.

PENCIL SHARPENERS

A schoolroom staple for more than 100 years, sharpeners are now a hot collectible. The iconic Boston KS and the Chicago-made APSCO (Automatic Pencil Sharpener Co.) Giant, above, are from 1930-1960.

FLASH CARDS

In addition to making phonics and vocabulary fun, vintage flash cards make great wall decor when framed singly or in groups. (Consider photocopying your cards to preserve the originals.) This set by McCormick–Mathers Publishing Co. of both Wichita, Kansas, and Columbus, Ohio, was produced in the 1950s.

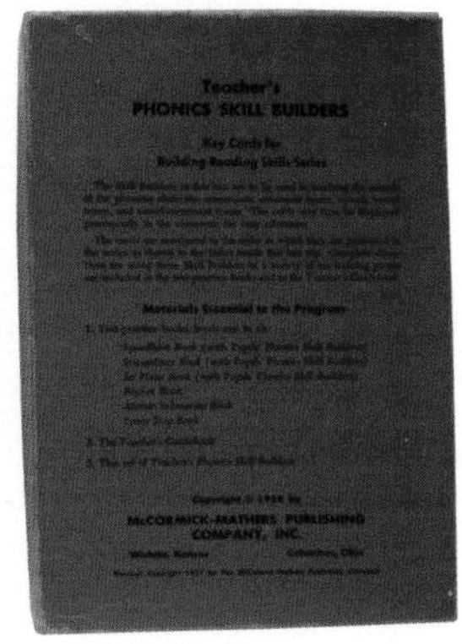

ALL SCHOOL ITEMS: JACKSON L. GARRISON

DESK

Decorating trends like industrial and steampunk have made school furniture popular in the home. This cast-iron and wood desk was produced by Peabody School Furniture Co. in North Manchester, Indiana, from 1900-1930.

High Notes

Take a cue from an antiques expert on these old-time musical instruments.

BY JOE KENZ

MELLOPHONE

Similar to a French horn but lighter and easier to play, mellophones are a favorite in concert and marching bands. C.G. Conn of Elkhart, Indiana, produced this model, now with a patina, in the 1920s-30s.

MANDOLIN

Widely known manufacturers such as Gibson and Martin made many of these string instruments, but this look-alike was created by the Chicago-based Lyon & Healy Co. Dating to the early 1900s, this mandolin is missing a string, which slightly affects its collector value.

GUITAR BANJO

With six strings instead of a normal banjo's four or five, a guitar banjo produces a much louder sound. These were often used as rhythm instruments in minstrel and Dixieland bands. Lyon & Healy Co. made this particular piece around 1920.

UKELIN

Considered to be novelty instruments, these violin-ukulele hybrids can be played with a bow or by plucking the strings. The International Music Co. of Hoboken, New Jersey, made this one around 1910. The fading graphics on this example alter its collector value.

MUSIC NOTES: TARCHYSHNIK ANDREI/SHUTTERSTOCK; BRASS AND STRINGS: JACKSON L. GARRISON

TUNE UP YOUR HOME

No matter their value, old instruments always have tons of decorating potential. Add vintage vibrations to any space with these fun ways to display them.

- **Hang found violins** or guitars on a wall—alone or in multiples—to make a stunning statement.
- **Repurpose an instrument** to create one-of-a-kind lighting and furniture. Consider wiring that trumpet to make a lamp or converting a drum into a side table.
- **Frame sheet music** and piano rolls. You can also use them to line dresser drawers or to craft flowers, wreaths and table runners.
- **Gather smaller instruments,** such as harmonicas or whistles, to display in a tabletop arrangement or in a shadow box.

ACCORDION

Most likely manufactured in the 1950s when the accordion craze swept the country, this learner instrument was produced in Italy and distributed under the United brand by Don Noble Co. of Chicago. Today's polka, zydeco and Tejano bands opt for more expensive models with higher-quality metal reeds.

LICENSING BY WHEATIES

In 1953, a box of Wheaties cereal contained a small license plate, approximately 2 by 5 inches.

After collecting six of these license plates, I sent in six box tops and $2 for a deal offered on the back of the box. I received plates for all 48 states, the U.S. territories, 10 Canadian provinces and 13 countries (some are above).

What's amazing to me is not that I collected these miniature license plates but that I have kept them all these years!

JOHN MILLSAPPS
WINDSOR, COLORADO

A Read on Children's Books

Here's the story on what makes kiddie lit collectible.

BY BARBARA J. EASH

THE QUARREL

My little old man and I fell out;
I'll tell you what 'twas all about,—
I had money and he had none,
And that's the way the noise begun.

THE PUMPKIN-EATER

Peter, Peter, pumpkin-eater,
Had a wife and couldn't keep her;
He put her in a pumpkin shell,
And there he kept her very well.

TONGS

Long legs, crooked thighs,
Little head, and no eyes.

JACK JINGLE

Little Jack Jingle,
He used to live single;
But when he got tired of this
kind of life,
He left off being single and
lived with his wife.
Now what do you think of
little Jack Jingle?
Before he was married he used
to live single.

98

Stories live so close to our hearts that if I asked you to name your favorite childhood books, you could probably rattle them off instantly, even if it's been years since you read them.

From *Little Women* to the *Little House* books, familiar characters and stories have endured, some for generations.

A book's value depends on several factors. Is it a first or limited edition? Was it signed by the author? Is it illustrated, and are the illustrations very appealing? Is the subject matter of wide interest, or specialized?

"First edition" generally refers to the books printed from one continuous operation of the press. Different publishing houses use different means to identify their first editions, sometimes simply putting the words on the copyright page. If there's a date on the title page, it must match the copyright date, with no other date listed.

Book club editions are generally of lower quality, and not as sought after.

For autographed and inscribed items, collectors will want to verify the signature; genuine signatures tend to increase a book's value.

Collectors seek books in "fine" or "very good" condition, with intact spines and no major defects. (All defects should be listed and described when selling a book).

Of course, a child's book is often wrinkled, torn or scribbled in—it was made not to sit on the shelf but to be handled, hugged and lugged around. Children's books that have been treated that way are usually in such poor condition that they'll never have a high dollar value—but to the owners, they're priceless nonetheless.

DAY IN AND DAY OUT WORKBOOK ›

Publishing houses brought out their own reading primers, complete with teacher's guides and workbooks. This 1957 workbook was used with the *Day In and Day Out* first-grade primer from the Alice & Jerry Basic Reading Program, offering practice exercises and quizzes. This one was never completed; even the name line on the back cover remains blank.

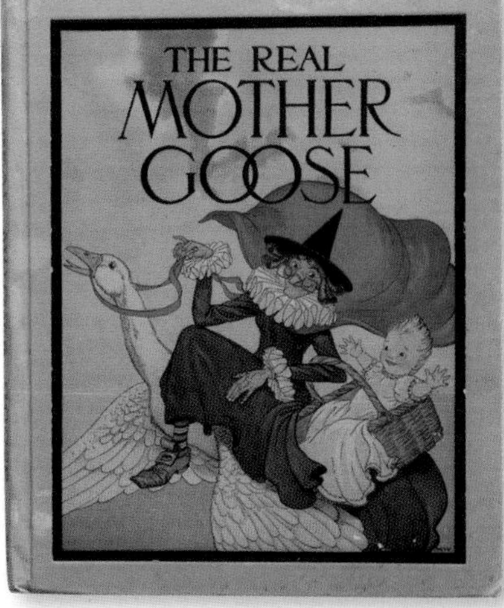

‹ *THE REAL MOTHER GOOSE*

There are countless collections of the nursery rhymes and children's tales many of us know by heart. This 1942 edition, with a copyright date of 1916, features pen and watercolor illustrations by Blanche Fisher Wright. Reprinted many times, it's one of the best-selling children's books of all time.

DICK AND JANE, THE CLASSIC PRIMERS ›

Zerna Sharp, a teacher and reading consultant, helped millions of children learn to read through this celebrated series, used in classrooms from 1927 through the 1970s. She developed the idea for a primer that introduced no more than one word on each page, and no more than five new words in each story. Colorful illustrations helped young readers stay interested. These are 1985 reproductions.

THE BOBBSEY TWINS: ON AN AIRPLANE TRIP

This series about a family with two pairs of boy-girl twins ran between 1904 and 1979. Edward Stratemeyer, one of publishing's most successful entrepreneurs, saw an untapped market for children's books; he wrote the first under the name Laura Lee Hope. Like his other series—including Nancy Drew and the Hardy Boys, published under the umbrella of the Stratemeyer Syndicate—this one was written by a variety of authors using a single pen name. Updates took the stories from horse-and-carriage days through international jet travel; publishers used a variety of formats. This 1933 Grosset & Dunlap volume, with dust jacket, is in average condition.

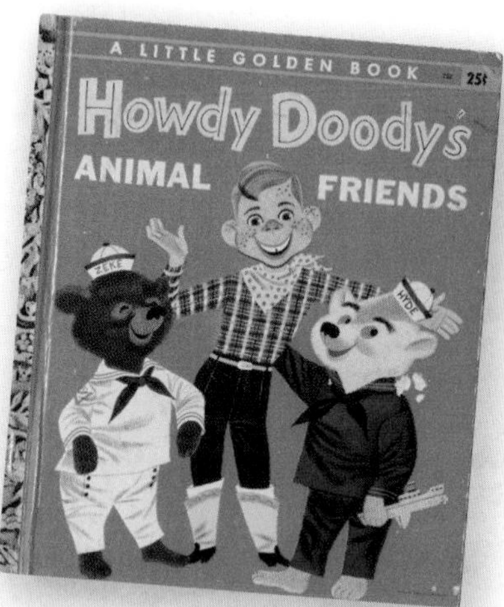

HOWDY DOODY'S ANIMAL FRIENDS

The first 12 Little Golden Books, including *The Poky Little Puppy*, came out in 1942. Noted for their distinctive, colorful look and reasonable prices (they first sold for 25 cents), the books eventually sold more than 2 billion copies. Some stories featured figures from popular culture, like this one about Howdy Doody, the freckled marionette from the 1947-60 children's TV show.

THE CORNER HOUSE GIRLS: ON A HOUSEBOAT

Another Stratemeyer Syndicate product, this 1915-26 series chronicled the lives of four orphaned sisters who move into a house left to them by a wealthy great-uncle. Its front covers remained identical throughout; finding all 13 volumes would be quite a feat. Each sold for a then-hefty price of 75 cents.

BARB'S TIPS FOR GOOD BOOK HEALTH

PROTECT THE SPINE
Keep books upright on a shelf or lying flat, never leaning. Never force books onto an overcrowded shelf.

CONTROL THE CLIMATE
Never store books on the floor of a damp basement, garage or storage unit; it's best to keep them where there is central heat and air conditioning. Moisture—even in the air—leads to foxing, a speckled discoloration of the pages.

KEEP THE DUST JACKET
Even with rips and other flaws, the jacket can triple the price a collector will pay.

HANDLE WITH CARE
Dust regularly with the soft brush on your vacuum cleaner. Use clean hands when reading and mark your place with a flat bookmark—never dog-ear the pages.

THE BUMPER BOOK

In the late 1970s, I bought this beautifully illustrated book, which was published in 1946, at a book sale. It attracted my attention because I was beginning my career as an elementary school teacher. I've since had the binding repaired, but the rest of the book is in its original condition. I have cherished *The Bumper Book* for decades. It is full of nice stories, rhymes and poems to read—it's unique!

SUZANNE MOFFITT • SOUTH BEND, IN

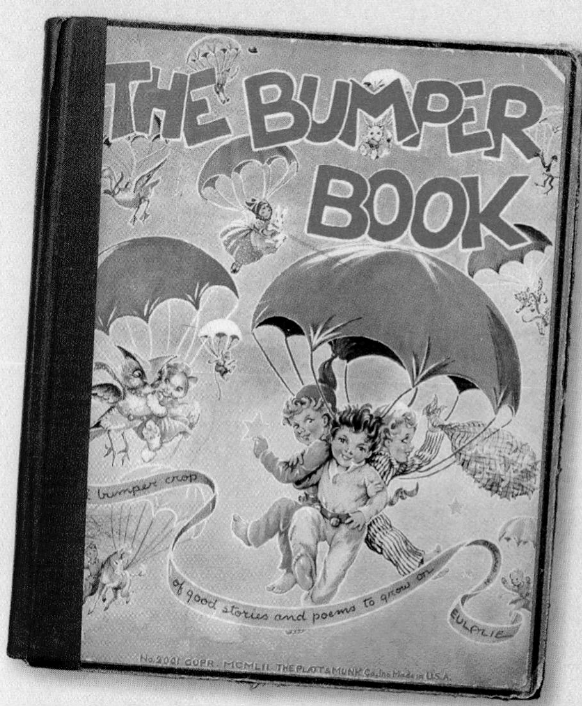

GOOD VS. EVIL

Every hero has a nemesis. Check out these famous comic book face-offs.

CAPTAIN AMERICA VS. RED SKULL

A Nazi agent trained by Hitler, Red Skull actually spurred the U.S. government to create Captain America. Equipped with combat skills, Red Skull often uses a trademark weapon: the Dust of Death.

SPIDER-MAN VS. THE GREEN GOBLIN

After Norman Osborn, the father of Peter Parker's real-life pal Harry, discovers a powerful elixir, the faltering industrialist becomes an insane supervillain. The Goblin later poses an added threat when he discovers Spider-Man's true identity.

FANTASTIC FOUR VS. DOCTOR DOOM

This classmate of brainy Reed "Mr. Fantastic" Richards is disfigured by his own supernatural lab machinery. After a plot to reach the spirit of his deceased mother—a witch—fails, he abuses his power in pursuit of world domination.

X-MEN VS. MAGNETO

Magneto isn't inherently evil. But the Holocaust survivor, whose deadly strikes against anti-mutant society are often all about payback, constantly has to be stopped from inciting mass violence and deeper social divides.

THOR VS. LOKI

The god of thunder's troublesome adoptive brother—the god of mischief himself—jealously schemes against his sibling, with endless evil plots, attack goons and attempts to discredit Thor in the eyes of their powerful father, Odin.

LEFT: MARVEL ENTERTAINMENT, LLC (5)

THE PERFECT AGE TO START

SOON AFTER WE MOVED from Minneapolis to Chicago's north side, I set out on a summer day to explore my new surroundings. Venturing into an alley down the block, I spotted a strange item lying on the ground. It was a comic book.

As an 8-year-old boy, I'd never seen a comic book before, but *The Amazing Spider-Man* grabbed my attention with its colorful cover. The drawings inside came to life and the characters seemed to leap off the pages as I read about Spider-Man's adventures. I was hooked! In fact, I was so lost in this fantastic new world that I cut my bare foot on a piece of glass as I ambled home, never taking my eyes off those pages.

That Spider-Man comic book—issue No. 33, "The Final Chapter"—is now a classic. One of Marvel's greatest tales, the story pits Spidey against Doctor Octopus. In mint condition, this issue might be worth hundreds of dollars today. But as a kid, I never imagined the collectible value of these books; I just wanted to read the stories.

Month after month, I read about all the Marvel characters: the Fantastic Four, the X-Men, Captain America, Iron Man, Thor, Daredevil, the Hulk, the Sub-Mariner—the list seemed to go on and on. Soon one comic turned into a stack, which multiplied into boxes and boxes.

All these years later, I still have many of those comics. Someday I hope to pass on the excitement I discovered in their pages.

PRESTON CLAY FAWCETT
RACINE, WI

Comic books captured the imagination of Preston (in pink shirt at top right) as a kid in the 1960s. These days, the Marvel devotee still has many of his treasured childhood comics (above), hoping to one day share the adventures with a new fan.

YOUNG AVENGERS

BLOCKBUSTER MOVIES based on Marvel comic book characters remind me of those never-ending summer days when I was 10, playing with my three best friends, imagining ourselves as The Avengers.

My pal Clary (none of us called him by his given name, Clarence) often called dibs on Thor, leaving Steve, Randy and me to argue about which superhero we would play.
My favorite was Spider-Man. As one of the smaller kids in my neighborhood, I felt a bit inadequate and could relate to awkward teen Peter Parker. But as Spider-Man, I could fly through the air and fight crime anonymously.

Our favorite place for adventures stood on the outskirts of town: several acres of pine trees, great for climbing. Next to the forest stood the town dump, ringed with heaps of sand dunes from which Spidey could jump—or, rather, swing—to the rescue. The only mishap I remember was Iron Man's suit failing and Randy ending up at the doctor's office. His broken arm eventually mended, but his mom wasn't too thrilled with our adventures.

Those were the days, playing heroes and protecting our little corner of the world from evildoers. Whenever we took a break from fighting crime, we'd run to the dime store to buy another comic, which offered yet another story to fuel our thrilling exploits.

I may have hung up my imaginary Spidey suit, but I'll never forget my days as an Avenger, battling villains and saving the world.
PHIL BARTELME • WEST ALLIS, WI

Young Phil looked unassuming in his school photo, but after school he turned into an Avenger.

VINTAGE READS

EVEN MONSTERS HAVE A GOOD SIDE

Comic book fans met an angry new face in May 1962.

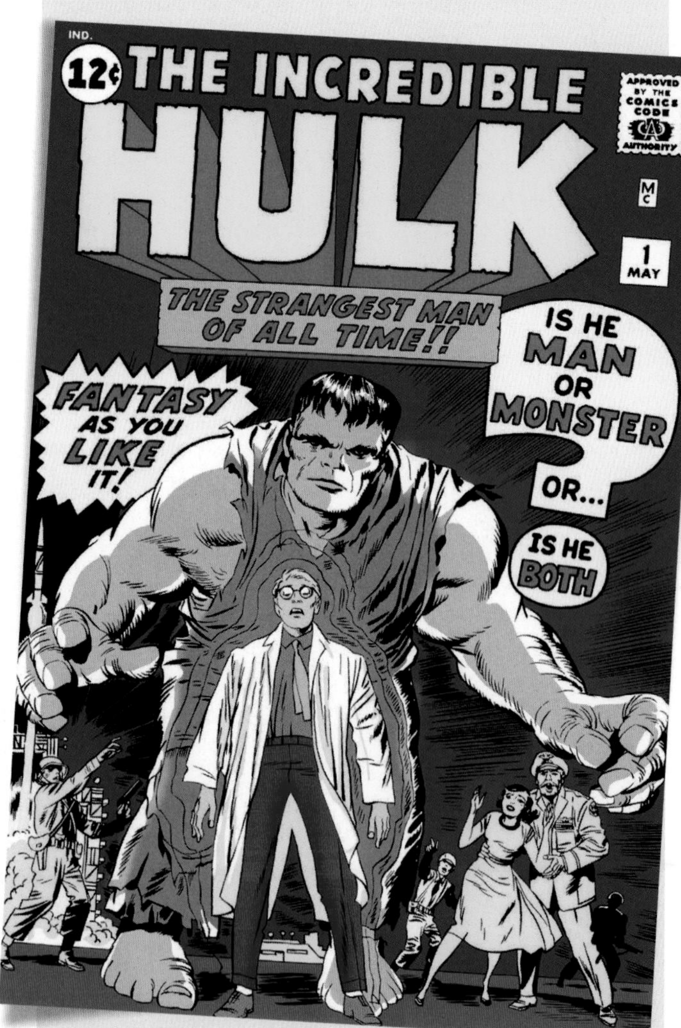

HERO OR VILLAIN?
The storyline of Bruce Banner and his angry alter ego, the Hulk was created by Stan Lee and Jack Kirby. *The Incredible Hulk No. 1* introduced the big gray brute, who became the now-familiar green in issue No. 2.

VINTAGE

ADS

SEND NO MONEY!

X-ray specs, dog whistles, sea monkeys and a Charles Atlas body—every kid knew there was more to a comic book than the comics. The real excitement happened in the ads.

1962

Throw your voice into trunks, behind doors, everywhere. Instrument fits in your mouth and out of sight. Fool teacher, friends and family. Free book on "How to Become a Ventriloquist." No. 2137.....25¢

SILENT DOG WHISTLE
This whistle can't be heard by human ears, but Rover can hear it half a mile away. Your dog will understand that this whistle is for him alone. Be amazed how quickly he responds.
No. 3781 $1.00

MUSICAL JUKE BOX BANK
Drop in a coin and the turntable revolves to a lilting melody ...just like the modern juke box that youngsters adore. Makes saving a pleasure—money mounts up. Made of sturdy metal. 4½"x4".
No. 2005.... $1.50

DRAW OR PAINT ANYTHING IN ONE MINUTE
Amazing new art reproducer actually reflects any indoor or outdoor scene you wish to draw on any paper. Simply follow the line of your picture image, and presto! A beautiful drawing is yours.
No. 3306 ...... $1.98

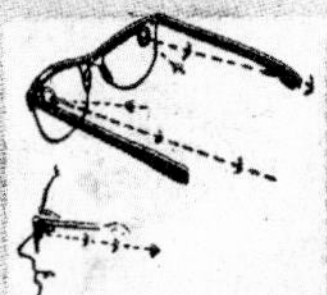

SEE BEHIND GLASSES
A specially treated pair of sunglasses with secret mirrors that enable you to see behind you, without anyone knowing your watching. Really comes in handy at times.
8030 75¢

YOU, TOO, CAN BE TOUGH
Master Jui Jitsu and you'll win any fight. This book gives all the grips, blocks, etc which are so effective in counterattack. FREE book on how to perform strong man stunts also included.
NO. 224 .... 1.00

SURPRISE PACKAGE
Are you willing to take a chance? We won't tell you what you get, but because you're willing to gamble, we'll give you more than your money's worth.
No. 678........ Only 50¢

AMAZING MINIATURE RADIO
This tiny, feather weight radio operates without batteries, without tubes, but brings you years of listening pleasure. There's nothing to wear out, nothing to replace.
No. 3044 $4.98

TREASURE CHEST OF FUN

TRANSISTOR RADIO KIT
This amazing radio kit contains all the components to construct a powerful, highly efficient instrument. It operates 1,000 hours on 2 junior pen light batteries and is simple to construct. Full instructions and all parts are included for you to build your own private transistor radio.
No. 2151 .... $5.98

KRAZY KRAX
Apply this to the television screen and it appears that the glass is cracked.
No. 3333 .60c

BANK VAULT WITH ALARM
Bank vault has combination type lock that gives an alarm when opened. Protects valuables and possessions. Frighten off would be invaders of your privacy. Excellent for storing money, valuables, prizes.
No. 2113 .... $1.49

BIKE WINDSHIELD
Turn your bike into something really special with this clear, transparent bike windshield. Just like the one on Motorcycles. Handy built-in pouch enables you to keep your sunglasses, tools, and personal effects within easy reach. Really makes your bike different.
No. 4268 .... $1.00

INSECT COLLECTING KIT
Complete equipment for making perfect safe, insect specimens. SET includes efficient net for catching insect, "killing jar", forceps, magnifying glass, mounting pins, preserving strips, identification labels, etc. Full instructions are included.
No. 2117 ....1.00

MINIATURE SECRET CAMERA
.... 1.25

EXPLODING HAND GRENADE
This menacing hand grenade looks and works just like a real one. All you do is pull the pin, throw the grenade, and watch the fun as the caps explode. It's harmless.
2109 .... 75¢

Sorry, but we cannot ship orders totalling less than $1.00" Kindly add 15¢ for postage and handling to all orders.

BIKE SPEEDOMETER
Now you can see how fast you're riding with this precision engineered speedometer for only 75¢. You can time yourself for racing, sports, distance. Just fasten it to your handlebar and go.
No. 8199 .... 75¢

HONOR HOUSE PROD. CORP., Dept. GK-58 LYNBROOK, N.Y.
Rush me the items listed below. If I am not 100% satisfied, I may return any part of of my purchase after 10 days Free Trial for full refund of purchase price.

ITEM #	NAME OF ITEM	HOW MANY	TOTAL PRICE

☐ I enclose .... in full payment. Same guarantee.
☐ Send C.O.D. I will pay postman on delivery plus postage.

Name...

Address..

CANADIAN FRIENDS: For quick service, send orders directly to:
NEW YORK IMPORTS BOX 121 DOWNSVIEW, TORONTO

AMAZING NEW SPACE PHONE SET — 2 WAY . . SENDS . . . RECEIVES
You can talk back and forth between houses, from room to room, and from secret hiding places, because it's portable - no electric wires - no batteries.
No. 3184 .... .69c

ATOMIC SMOKE BOMB
Just light one and watch the column of thick, white smoke rise to the ceiling, mushrooming into a dense cloud, just like an A-Bomb.
No. 971........................20¢

This "treasure chest of fun" ran in the back of Marvel's *Tales to Astonish* Vol. 1, No. 36, published in October 1962.

It Was All She Talked About

Chatty Cathy spoke to her heart long after childhood.

My favorite doll as a kid was a real chatterbox: Chatty Cathy, the toy sensation of the early 1960s. I loved Cathy and her repertoire of almost a dozen observations and musings: "I'm hungry," "I'm tired," "Let's play house!" In the days before the computer chip, Cathy was able to chat thanks to a small recorder activated by a pull string at the back of her neck.

I not only loved Cathy, I coveted her. My mom balked at the price tag, which was high at the time.

"I'm not spending $18 on a doll," she told me. And it didn't matter how much I begged, which was a lot.

It was lucky for me that a friend down the street had a grandma who was more than willing to shell out for such a marvel, so off to her house I would go for pull-string magic.

I'm embarrassed to say that I didn't let go of my Cathy-envy for quite some time. In my teens, I continued to tease my mom about the longed-for doll that never came my way. Mom was good enough to laugh about it.

But that isn't the end of the story. Chatty Cathy was a topic of conversation for me well into adulthood. I almost talked my husband's ear off with tales of the $18 wonder that was beyond my childhood grasp.

Amazingly, he was listening. One Christmas morning, with my 6-year-old daughter watching, I unwrapped a big present with my name on it.

I didn't let go of my Cathy-envy for quite some time.

And there she was: Chatty Cathy, a replica of the original doll now marketed for wistful baby boomers like me.

I was thrilled, and eager to share her with my daughter. Together we pulled the string. "I love you," Cathy warbled in her peculiar crackly pitch. My daughter winced. "Too scary," she declared.

So Chatty Cathy went back into her box, where she's stayed ever since, albeit in a place of honor in my closet. Scary or no, I still love her.

MARY VALLO • PEARL RIVER, NY

DOLLS THROUGH THE DECADES

1920s

Johnny Gruelle's publisher first sells **Raggedy Ann Dolls** and books in 1918; **Raggedy Andy** appears in 1920.

1930s

After 20 prototypes, the **Shirley Temple Doll** hits shelves in 1934. The smallest sells for $3, or $56 in today's money.

1940s

Hedwig Dolls, based on Marguerite de Angeli's children's stories, are a hit, with nine dolls in the series.

1950s

1959 ushers in **Barbie**, who has girls expanding their worlds and imagining the pursuit of careers outside the home.

1960s

Chatty Cathy talks back, and girls love it. **G.I. Joe**, the first "action figure," is popular for boys.

1970s

Star Wars figures become hot-ticket collectibles.

1980s

Each **Cabbage Patch Doll** comes with a birth certificate and adoption papers.

PLAYING HOUSE

Kids have been playing with dolls since at least Roman times, and for good reason: to love a doll is to learn the value of caring for others. A dollhouse teaches us the power of imagination—not to mention how the right wallpaper can really transform a room.

LITTLE DREAM HOME

Mother ordered this dollhouse for me when I was 3, after she heard an offer on a radio program. I diligently cared for it and kept it in pristine condition.

MANETTA BURGERMEISTER • MUSKEGO, WI

TINY TEARS BRINGS CRIES OF JOY

I have home movies of getting my Tiny Tears doll on Christmas Day in 1959. I was so excited, I could've done commercials for the doll company. Here we are on my fourth birthday, in 1960.

CONNIE CONNELY • TULSA, OK

OUT FOR A STROLL

Here I am giving my baby doll a ride in her carriage in 1955.

ALICE SCHEFFELL CLARK • JACKSONVILLE, FL

Susie hugs Teddy as sister Judy reads another thrilling tale. Their brother Fred is doing his best to ignore them.

Teddy to the Rescue

When the story gets scary, a cuddle works wonders.

When I was 8 and my sister Susie (now she's Suzanne) was 5, I liked to read stories to her. I had a talent for the dramatic, so when I read a story such as "The Three Billy Goats Gruff" or something from *Grimm's Fairy Tales*, I used my scariest voice for the sheer pleasure of frightening her.

If Mom was in the room, she'd say, "Tone it down, Judy, you're going to give your sister nightmares." But that didn't stop me from reading Susie the scariest stories again.

During these readings, our brother Fred would pretend he wasn't listening, Mom would be busy crocheting and Dad would be reading the newspaper with our dog sleeping in his lap. This was the usual nightly scene in our home back in 1948.

One evening while we were reading our bedtime story, Mom surprised my sister with a homemade teddy bear she had been working on for several weeks. It was supposed to be for Susie's birthday, but I guess Mom couldn't wait any longer to give it to her.

I had already graduated from cuddly teddy bears to storybook dolls, so I wasn't hurt when I didn't get one. Still, as teddy bears go, this was one of the cutest I had ever seen.

From that day on, my little sister never put that bear down unless it was bath time. He was in her arms during story time, nap time, bedtime and any other time she could drag him around with her. He was her pal during the day and her comfort at night.

Amazingly, Teddy still lives, though he suffered miserably at the hands (or paws) of various pets and Suzanne's three daughters, who loved him to pieces before he was carefully wrapped in tissue and retired to the attic.

One day Teddy will be no more, but one thing's for sure: He was the best toy a little girl could ever hope for. My sister will attest to that.

JUDY SIKORSKI • ROSSFORD, OH

BEAR NECESSITIES

One of the first toys a child receives, a teddy bear is also the first keeper of our secrets, the first to comfort us after a bad dream and the first guest at our tea parties. He is our first best friend.

STICKING WITH CINNAMON

My mother gave me Cinnamon Bear for Christmas in 1943, when I was 7. I loved him dearly. At 15, I moved by bus from California to Washington. There was no room in my suitcase for Cinnamon Bear, so he sat on my lap all the way to Seattle. I got some questioning looks, but I didn't care.

JERI MULLER
NEWCASTLE, CA

STEIFF'S 1-2-3s

1880
Margarete Steiff, a seamstress whose childhood polio left her unable to walk, establishes her toy company in Germany. Her first big seller is a felt elephant.

1892
The toy company catalog shows a line of felt toy animals that includes a monkey, dog and giraffe.

1902
Margarete's nephew Richard designs Bear 55PB, the world's first toy bear with moveable arms and legs. Instead of felt, it's covered in plush mohair—better for cuddling.

1906
3,000 bears, named Teddy Bears after President Theodore Roosevelt, hit the U.S. market. By 1907, Steiff has made close to 1 million toy Teddys.

2018
Steiff designs include Bobby the Blue-Footed Booby.

Gifts That Run On Fun

One beloved set of trucks rolls through generations.

As a young boy growing up in the early '50s, my life was not always easy, and toys were scarce for me and my siblings. Our dad worked hard as a machinist, but he had an uphill battle trying to keep the bills paid and food on the table for our family of seven.

My sister Barbara had been born with a heart defect. Her condition required surgery when she was 12 and again when she was 16, and those medical bills kept Dad so busy he had to work two jobs.

I had three brothers, one of them my identical twin, Ron. Ron and I often got one toy to share between us at Christmas. The upside was that we always appreciated the toys we received and took very good care of them.

Over the years we accumulated several nice toys, including a Buddy L farm supplies dump truck, a red flatbed truck with a blue steam shovel and a few TootsieToy cars. Ron and I spent wonderful long summer days building tiny roads for our toy trucks in the family's gravel driveway. Our mailman would pause on his route each day and smile as he watched us play.

One day he came back with a special surprise for us—a big load of toy trucks his own son had outgrown. Among them were a road grader, an excavator, a dump truck, a tow truck, a cement mixer and two flatbed semitrailer trucks.

Those toys provided hours of enjoyment. When we outgrew them, Mom put them away, thinking that we might have our own children one day, when the trucks would be put to good use again.

In the years since, the toys have entertained my son and later, my two older grandsons.

I still have the trucks and display some of them in my home; they so readily call to mind those endless summer days of my youth.

Through all these years, I have never forgotten the generosity and thoughtfulness of our mailman, whose gifts gave us cherished memories.

DONALD KRAMER
OSWEGO, IL

Tonka's founders took a chance on selling toys in 1947, after buying out a competitor. They sold 37,000 diggers and cranes that first year and never looked back.

RIGHT: CLASSICSTOCK/ALAMY STOCK PHOTO

VROOM-VROOM!

They're big and noisy and they look like dinosaurs—what child can resist construction equipment in action? The miniature versions have continued to fascinate children today almost as much as they did when they first became popular in the 1940s. Virginia Lee Burton captured the delight of watching machines at work in her 1939 book *Mike Mulligan and His Steam Shovel,* which, like toy trucks, remains a popular gift for kids.

HOLIDAY MEMENTOS

CHAPTER 7

The holidays are rooted in tradition and family fun. Let these vintage cards, platters, ornaments and more inspire you to look back fondly on your own special celebrations from years past.

HODGSON'S
QUIZZICAL
VALENTINE WRITER,
BEING A COLLECTION
OF NEW AND APPROPRIATE
VALENTINES,
SUITED TO ALL RANKS AND CONDITIONS
OF
QUIZZICAL LOVERS.

Collected and arranged by an eminent Quizzical Character.

LONDON:
ORLANDO HODGSON,
10, CLOTH FAIR, WEST SMITHFIELD.

③ **PERFECT VERSES** for valentines were suggested in booklets for lovers with no poetic flair.

Love Story

How to find the best match among a wealth of antique valentines.

BY SHARON SELZ

Vintage valentines make the heart of any card-carrying romantic beat faster, especially around Feb. 14. You gotta love 'em.

If you fancy anything old-fashioned and enjoy antiquing, consider bypassing the drugstore cards. The selection of vintage valentines is vast, and it isn't hard to find a treasure to send to someone special or to add to your own collection.

To get started, two not-so-secret admirers of antique valentines are here to help you find the perfect match for your interests: Nancy Rosin of Franklin Lakes, New Jersey, who heads the National Valentine Collectors Association, the Ephemera Society of America and *victoriantreasury.com*; and Shirley Burdick, a longtime valentine collector from Jefferson, Massachusetts.

① FOR THE CRAFTER

Before machines began turning out valentines in about 1880, cards were always handmade. The most creative ones were intricate and hand-cut, embroidered or painted, sometimes according to directions in magazines.

"Homemade valentines might have been decorated with whatever was at hand—pressed flowers, snippets of dress fabric, even locks of woven hair," Rosin explains. "The handcrafted pieces in my personal collection are among my favorites. I like to think of actual people making them by candlelight."

② FOR THE ROMANTIC

Have a soft spot for elegant tokens of love? Thank Esther Howland, sometimes called "the mother of the American valentine." The industry she invented in the mid-1800s turned romance into a booming business.

"I'm infatuated with Howland's valentines," says Burdick, who owns some rare and highly prized pieces. "Her Victorian designs featured embossed flowers, imported lace paper, gilt paper and often five or six layers." Lovers lifted flaps, pulled tabs and opened windows until they discovered a message—or perhaps even an engagement ring in a hidden compartment.

"The demand for Howland's cards was so great that she recruited friends to put them together," Burdick adds, noting that Howland used an assembly line long before Henry Ford did. A savvy

PREVIOUS SPREAD, ORNAMENTS: WILLIAM OGDEN; KIDS: ADVERTISING ARCHIVE/COURTESY businesswoman, she developed both simple cards that sold for 5 cents and highly elaborate lace paper confections that sold for an astonishing $50—as much as a fine buggy.

3 FOR THE POET

Long before Hallmark, suitors of the 18th and 19th centuries could find a "valentine writer" at their local bookseller. These handy pamphlets provided the tongue-tied with tasteful, comic or sugary verses. Howland offered a book of 131 sayings, Burdick says, so customers could find just the right one to inscribe on a homemade card. There were even responses for women to send back to their beaux, either politely encouraging or poetically rejecting them.

4 FOR THE PRACTICAL JOKER

Far from lovey-dovey, the comic "penny dreadfuls" of the 19th century were the original anti-valentine. Also known as "vinegar valentines," they usually aimed a satiric dart at a recipient's occupation, appearance or behavior. "They were made on cheap paper and were often insulting—not the kind of valentine people held on to as keepsakes," Rosin notes. A card might slyly lull the recipient with a pretty cover message like "You have such a face…" before it delivered the inside zinger "…that only a mother could love."

5 FOR THE HISTORIAN

Some valentines even bring great events of the past to vivid life. "During the Civil War, valentines were a tender link to home that gave the troops the will to go on," Rosin says. Some featured flags, battlefield tents or pictures of soldiers with their sweethearts.

The women's suffrage movement inspired an avalanche of 1916 valentines to President Woodrow Wilson and members of Congress, with such bold messages as "Love me. Love my vote."

"Card-makers were always trying to keep a step ahead of customers, picking up on inventions and trends," Rosin says. As cars were mass-produced at the turn of the 20th century, valentines pictured couples in cars. In the 1950s, space exploration was conveyed with couples aboard moon-bound rocket ships.

Both Burdick and Rosin appreciate today's instant e-cards as one more clever way valentines keep evolving. But they still believe the paper ones pull more powerfully on the heartstrings.

1 EARLY AMERICAN valentines were handmade, like this paper-cut *scherenschnitte* card circa 1825.

2 FANTASY AND ROMANCE are at the heart of cards by Esther Howland, who popularized Valentine's Day greetings in 19th-century America.

4 COMIC VALENTINES, decorated with caricatures, weren't so funny to the parties they targeted.

5 THE TENT opens to show the image of a Civil War soldier in 1863 writing to the beloved he left behind.

Greeting card giant Hallmark began selling valentines in 1916. The company shared these gems from the 1920s (right) and 1940s (left).

Be Mine, Valentine

These vintage treasures keep the romance alive.

Sweethearts have expressed their love in letters and handmade greetings for centuries, but it wasn't until the mid-1800s that early card companies started playing matchmaker. After the U.S. Postal Service introduced postcards, commercial valentines really took off, gaining popularity in the early 1900s.

Often featuring illustrations of new technologies, including cameras, radios and typewriters, these cutesy cards drew inspiration from the times.

"Valentines were an eye on what was going on in society," says Nancy Rosin, president of the National Valentine Collectors Association. "Card-makers took advantage of what was popular, whether it was comic books or cars."

Vintage valentines still delight many collectors and loved ones who have saved old cards as romantic keepsakes.

"You can hold them in your hand and cherish them for years," Rosin says.

Here are some favorite love notes from the past that celebrate the fun and romance of Valentine's Day.

1

2

3

4

5

LOVE ABOUNDS

Fall head over heels for these cherished valentines preserved through the years.

1 A tricycle built for two, decade unknown.
2 Girlish greeting, 1920s.
3 Message from the rooster, 1940s.
4 Lovely embossed postcard, 1910s.
5 Hopeful hearts, 1930s.

CONSIDERING COLLECTING?

Get started with tips from Nancy Rosin and the National Valentine Collectors Association:

- Find vintage valentines on eBay and at paper shows, antique shops, estate sales and flea markets. They're often hidden in boxes of old postcards or photos.
- Consider joining the National Valentine Collectors Association (*valentinecollectors.com*) or the Ephemera Society of America (*ephemerasociety.org*) once you get started. The latter deals with paper collectibles of every kind, from advertisements to posters to theater tickets.
- Check out your dealer. Though prices range from a quarter to hundreds of dollars, don't spend big bucks without first ensuring that the dealer is a reputable one who will stand behind his or her merchandise and accept returns.
- Store with TLC. Keep these treasures away from sunlight in acid-free containers, which are easy to find in scrapbooking supply stores. Look for the words "acid free" or "archival quality" on the labels.
- Understand pricing. Dollar value depends on a card's condition, rarity, artwork, desirability and sometimes the reputation of its designer or artist. Three-dimensional valentines and those with movable parts, called mechanicals, are often worth more.
- Learn more. Look for books or online articles by experts. Visit museums, which periodically offer displays and also may bring valentine collections out on request.

'I WISH YOU LUCK'

On St. Patrick's Day, friends and family often sent blessings to each other via postcard. These vintage cards bring not only a smile, but also the luck of the Irish.

This postcard, circa 1908, is masculine themed with an emerald green top hat, matching gloves and a clay pipe.

St. Patrick himself is shown here with a small shamrock in his right hand, and a large one placed directly behind him.

A sweet little boy smiles in this circa 1918 postcard illustrated by Ellen Clapsaddle.

A delightful rosy-cheeked Irish girl dressed in green and white fronts this postcard. She's holding up a handful of shamrocks.

The men in this antique postcard are seen toasting the shamrock while dressed in their finest attire for the occasion. The green chairs are a nice touch.

The harp is a symbol of Ireland, and is often associated with decorations for the holiday.

A young woman sitting inside a shamrock, gently holding the same in her hands, certainly says happy St. Patrick's Day.

"The Lady of Ireland to-day is seen On St. Patrick's Day in the Morning," says this greeting. She seems to fully represent the holiday spirit.

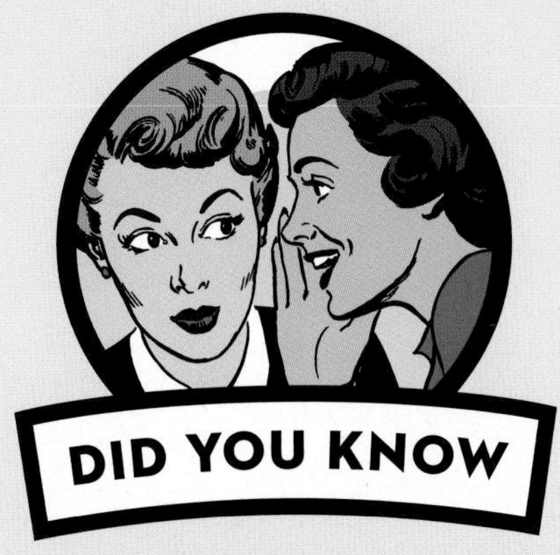

DID YOU KNOW

ERIN GO BRAGH
IS OFTEN TRANSLATED AS "IRELAND FOREVER."

Birds of a Feather

I have an impressive collection of Thanksgiving tableware, including 30 dinner plates and 15 sets of salt and pepper shakers, lining a wall of my basement. I also have separate displays of centerpiece turkeys and Degenhart glass turkey covered dishes.

My collection started with a plush turkey by Steiff, which I bought in Bad Hersfeld, Germany, while stationed there in 1955. It cost the equivalent of about $1.25. Today, a Steiff turkey can sell for quite a bit more.

As extensive as my collection is now, it used to be larger. When we downsized to a condo years ago, I parted with 35 sets of salt and pepper shakers. Shown here are a few favorite platters.

JIM NORTON • WOOSTER, OH

AUTUMN BEAUTY
This Spode pattern depicts a traditional pastoral scene.

COBALT CLASSIC ›
A flow blue tom-and-hen design circa 1900, from an Ohio River maker.

‹ PRACTICAL STYLE
A Melmac server from the 1950s.

PLATTERS, EXCEPT TOP RIGHT: LOREN FEDOROWICZ

FOLK ART
This circa 1950 piece of Blue Ridge pottery evokes country charm.

The hairline crack is a tangible reminder of Uncle Willie.

PEWTER HEIRLOOM
A finely detailed embossed design from Wendell August Forge in Berlin, Ohio.

INTRICATE ARTWORK
A prized piece by famed ceramicist Clarice Cliff.

CRACKING GOOD FUN

YOU COULD ALWAYS EXPECT two things from Uncle Willie: full volume and high energy. Every visit was punctuated by his booming voice and irrepressible spirit. He was a table-pounder, a shouter and sharer, a man with a flair for the dramatic. No dinner with him was ever boring. I looked forward to him coming over every holiday.

My mother's turkey platter was a point of pride for her. She displayed it on top of our cabinet above the kitchen table when it wasn't in use. One summer day, my Uncle Willie sat at the kitchen table, gesturing and shouting as he always did, and when he came to a big point he wanted to make—*BAM!*—he thumped the table with his fist.

CRASH! The turkey platter came clattering down from its perch and landed right in front of Uncle Willie. The platter now had a hairline crack running from rim to rim. There was a brief beat of silence, and then we all started to chuckle. Willie apologized, but no one was too angry. After all, it had truly been an accident, and maybe the turkey platter wasn't ruined after all.

Uncle Willie has been gone for many years now, but we still use the turkey platter every year, crack and all. With its imperfections, the platter is even more special to our family—because in a way, it brings Willie back to us, still making his mark on every holiday dinner.

MARLIES PALKA • WYNANTSKILL, NY

READY FOR SOME TURKEY

THE KITCHEN TABLE was where all the behind-the-scenes prep was done for Thanksgiving—and where the dinner was served as well. I took this picture of my mom, Frances, and dad, Rudolph, in 1954 when I was 17. We lived in Chicago, Illinois, at the time.

I used floodlights because I couldn't afford a flash attachment for my Argus A2 35 mm camera. This one really turned out well—a Norman Rockwell for sure.

My dad had his tongue out, a habit when he was doing a difficult job. He was partially paralyzed on his left side as the result of a diving injury he sustained while serving as a Navy Seabee in World War II. He'd spent nine months in traction.

My father had enlisted, as most patriotic men did at that time, even though he had two deferments. But when Dad got out of the service, he wasn't able to get the same kind of job he had before his accident. For the longest time he even refused to apply for VA assistance.

We made do with the little we had while growing up. My mom was a good mother and cook, and we all pulled together as a family.

When my younger brother Rudolph saw this picture, he was so impressed that he had three 8-by-10 framed reprints made, one for himself and the other two as gifts for me and my youngest brother, John.

Looking back, this is a special memory of our parents. It's what Thanksgiving in America is all about—good times with family.

KENNETH J. KWILOSZ • TEMPE, AZ

These salt and pepper shakers have graced our Thanksgiving table since the 1950s. Our grandchildren love to see them every year.

ELLEN SCOTT • NAPLES, FL

TABLE'S SET!

My brother Paul waits by the table on Thanksgiving 1954 at our home in Elmira, New York. Our usual centerpiece, a wax turkey, holds the spot where the meat platter will sit. Mom had us make paper pilgrims (top right) and a log cabin (bottom center) while the turkey cooked.

TOM HUONKER • ROCHESTER, NY

VINTAGE GREETINGS

THANKSGIVING BY POST

Collectible postcards were the text messages of their day.

FROM 1907 TO 1925, America went wild for postcards; in 1908 alone, the U.S. Post Office reported delivering 678 million of them—at a time when the population numbered just 89 million!

Picture postcards today are primarily associated with travel. But at the height of the craze, cards were as likely to be illustrations as photos, and travel was just one theme. Others were holidays (like the Thanksgiving cards here), religious events, elections—even natural disasters.

True, the messages weren't private—and postmasters undoubtedly read them! But at just a penny to buy and another to send, no one seemed to care much about the lack of privacy and writing space.

People treated them like little gifts, mounting them in albums alongside treasured family photos. They displayed them in frames and even bought storage chests with pullout viewing drawers.

Embossed 1908 card features brilliant color, gold trim, a pair of turkeys and a giant pumpkin.

Colorful 1910 card features children frolicking with pumpkins under a turkey's watchful gaze.

Also appealing to doll collectors, this sweet card features an illustration by H.B. Griggs.

Undated card leaves no doubt as to which date is the most important in November!

THANKSGIVING CARDS: BARBARA EASH (4)

Walking in a Retro Wonderland

Homespun touches and a love for vintage fill this kitchen with good cheer.

BY RACHAEL LISKA

"Don't be afraid to mix and match old decor with new decor," Kristy says. That's Kristy and Corey at left.

ALL PHOTOS EXCEPT THE ROBBS: KRISTY ROBB/ *WWW.ROBBRESTYLE.COM*; ROBBS: SHERRI WILSON

You won't find glammed-up Christmas trees, pristine place settings or luxury holiday decor in the Robb house in Fowler, Indiana. But there's no shortage of thrifty treasures decking its halls. Retro has a home here, too, and it all comes together to create a look that feels like it's been curated for years. The truth is, it has.

Before creating the *robbrestyle.com* blog and online shop, which is inspired by old-style charm, Corey and Kristy Robb described themselves as "makers, DIYers and lovers of all things rusty." Their kitchen is truly a reflection of this passion for mingling precious tokens of the past with present-day finds and handmade touches.

"We have a very eclectic style," Kristy says. "Early in our home ownership days we discovered that we could upcycle vintage pieces into decor for a lot less than what we could buy new from a store. My entire kitchen remodel was largely inspired by old farmhouse beadboard that we reclaimed as a backsplash." Open shelving in galvanized metal is stocked with colorful bowls, mason jar glasses and other flea market finds that complete this showcase wall.

"I knew open shelves were going to be tricky," says Kristy. "But I also knew that's where I could incorporate color, so I found pretty red and aqua dishes to accent the gray. I use this color palette throughout the kitchen to create a cohesive look.

"The dishes are a bit chaotic and not perfectly stacked, which fits our lifestyle. And when we have guests over, everyone knows where the cups are," she adds. "I use the boxes to store other items that I don't use as frequently and to hide clutter."

Kristy loves it when her finds serve double duty as organizational solutions. "But you have to decorate with the things that make you happy. All of these items have a story to tell."

BRIGHT IDEAS!

- When it comes to holiday decorating, pick a color palette and stick to it. "Red and green aren't the only colors," Kristy says. "White can be festive and fun, especially when paired with trinkets in silver and aqua."
- "Only put out decorations that you truly love," suggests Kristy. "Items with that nostalgic feel remind me of Christmases past."
- Deck an old dollhouse with cotton snow, mini holiday lights, snow village trees, wreaths and a toy car. Kristy's dollhouse (top right) fits on her retro dinette table.

"I'm obsessed with pennants and loved the idea of using them to decorate a Christmas tree," Kristy says. "Soda crates are always around the house, so we stacked a few to create height. Then I wrapped the tree bottom with flannel."

Ellyn Scarlett of Elkhart, Indiana, received this adorable card in 1951.

Greetings of the Season

How much do we love Christmas cards? The Greeting Card Association says Americans buy about 1.5 billion Christmas cards every year, 10 times more than the next most popular greeting card, the valentine.

Let us celebrate the Christmas card in all its forms—thoughtful, decorative, whimsical and lovably corny. Included here is a brief history of holiday greetings, and examples of colorful cards from the 1940s through the 1970s. These cards were contributed by Ellyn Scarlett of Elkhart, Indiana; Jerry Fedorovich of Terryville, Connecticut; Bernice McCoy of Danville, Illinois; and Johnny Howlett of Pulaski, Virginia, along with an anonymous donor.

These cheery greetings of Christmases past are now ones we can all enjoy.

TIMELESS KEEPSAKES

By the 1940s, it was common to decorate with Christmas cards. Eager to create greetings suitable for display, printers used special techniques and finishes such as cutouts, die cuts, embossing, foil stamps, deckled edges, metallic ink and glitter. Some featured ties for hanging the card on the tree.

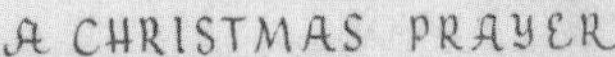

THE FIRST NOELS

HENRY COLE, an English civil servant with an interest in art, is credited with mailing the first mass-produced Christmas card in 1843. The story goes that with the holiday approaching, Cole was too busy to write individual greetings, so he thought of sending a general message.

Cole's friend and artist John Callcott Horsley did a sketch of a family celebrating their holiday dinner, captioned "A Merry Christmas and a Happy New Year to You." Cole had 1,000 cards printed (many were hand-colored), sending some and offering others for sale at a shilling each—about a week's pay for an average worker at the time.

The cards generated a backlash because Horsley's holiday sketch featured a woman helping a child to a tipple of Christmas wine.

Original Coles are collectibles; one sold for more than $28,000 in 2001.

Christmas cards caught on in the United States after 1875, when expert lithographer Louis Prang added them to his New England publishing business.

Within six years, Prang had a booming trade in holiday cards. He was producing 5 million a year, and his Roxbury, Massachusetts, factory was a tourist attraction.

Prang ran annual card-design competitions to promote the work of lesser-known artists, especially female painters. His cards were known for their quality, and many of them featured fringes, tassels and other embellishments.

The greeting card industry's annual design awards, The Louies, are named in honor of Prang.

> Grandma hung new and old Christmas cards and photos on ribbons next to her bed. She said they kept her family close as she read aloud to herself each night.
>
> **MERILEE BENGTSSON** • MUKILTEO, WA

IT'S SNOW FUN!
Whimsical, sentimental designs with cartoons in the 1950s and 1960s reflect Christmas becoming a more secular holiday focused on kids and gift-giving.

SPECIAL DELIVERIES
Publishers expanded their offerings in the 1960s and 1970s, with options for babies, teenagers and extended family members. They continued to experiment with graphic techniques, lettering and stylized designs.

1910

Hallmark Cards founder Joyce Hall was selling postcards out of a couple of shoeboxes. His brother Rollie soon joined him, followed a few years later by their brother William.

1915

In 1915, fire at their Kansas City, Missouri, store prompted the Halls to buy printing presses to make their own cards rather than import them from German printers, who dominated the market at the time.

The same year, the Hall brothers printed the world's first 4-by-6-inch folded Christmas card for mailing in an envelope.

1951

The first Hallmark Hall of Fame TV special, *Amahl and the Night Visitors*, aired live on NBC on Christmas Eve.

1960

Hallmark published Christmas cards designed by avant-garde artist Salvador Dali. But Dali's sketchy figures and bold splashes of color didn't appeal to holiday shoppers; Hallmark pulled the cards after a few weeks.

1963

Jacqueline Kennedy designed two Christmas cards for Hallmark to benefit what would become the Kennedy Center.

1977

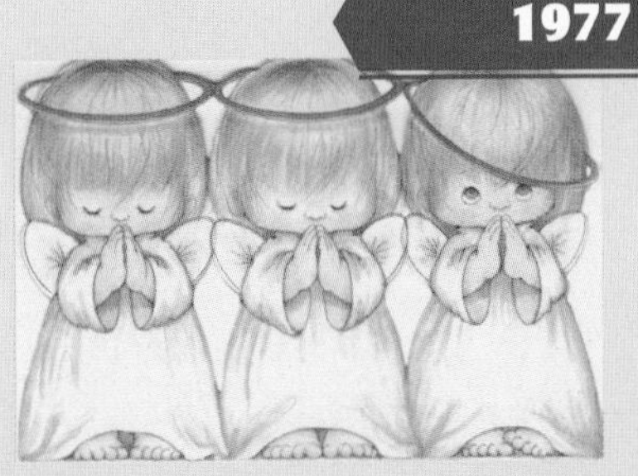

A Hallmark design known as Three Little Angels, of praying cherubs, one with her halo askew, is the most popular Christmas card in history. It's been sent more than 36 million times—and counting—since its introduction.

12 WAYS OF CHRISTMAS

A love affair with holiday wonder begins when we're young; the bite of the collector bug often comes much later.

1 ONE-OF-A-KIND ORNAMENTS

THANKS FOR THE MEMORIES

My mother, Anna M. Fischer McQuaid, was a saver and a collector. She kept beloved ornaments from Christmas trees at Dad's and her childhood homes, some of them with antique candleholders. After 1931, she added ornaments that she and Dad bought or their children and grandchildren made.

After our daughters were born in 1960 and 1970, I started buying special ornaments for them every year and putting them on our tree. I'd mark the year and the recipient on each ornament, forming a starter set for each daughter. Later, when they married and moved out, each received her own traditional ornament collection.

Just about that time, my mother started to sort through her prized collectibles to give to my siblings and me. I was blessed to receive more of them from one sibling who is not a saver.

Now each year, I choose a new selection of these fragile and beautiful ancestral ornaments to hang near the tiny white lights on my little tree. They give me such joy as I give thanks for my mother, the real collector of memories.

CAROLYN J. "CARI" THOMAS
SANTA BARBARA, CA

2 FEATHER TREE

ABSOLUTELY ORNAMENTAL

Antique glass ornaments hang from a 20-inch goose feather tree that my husband, Alec, and I display in our home at Christmastime. The collection includes family heirlooms from our grandparents, as well as antique-store purchases I've made over the years. The red and gold bell and light blue teardrop ornament in the upper center of the tree were brought to the United States by my grandmother, who emigrated from Germany around 1915.

SHARON CROMER • WEST COLUMBIA, SC

3 ANGELS

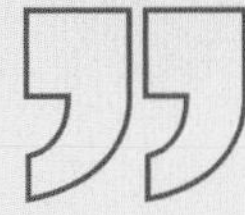

This little angel has been on my tree for more than 60 years. My mother said I picked her out when I was 5. Unfortunately, the hot bulbs of the 1950s burned her face, but I love her just the same.

CARMEN HOUSTON • PIEDMONT, SC

4 CERAMIC STATUES

CHRISTMAS YEAR-ROUND

I leave out these special Christmas collectibles all year. Most belonged to my grandmother Elaine Six, who passed away in 1970 at the age of 54. We called her Grandma Lane. She worked at the dime store in downtown Des Moines, and I'm sure that she accumulated them at after-holiday sales. It makes me happy to see them every day.

RONDA GARNETT • WEST DES MOINES, IA

Antique blown-glass ornaments originated in Germany. Artisans hand-painted them inside and out.

5

MASS-PRODUCED GLASS ORNAMENTS

BRITE WITH POSSIBILITIES

I have been collecting vintage Christmas tree ornaments for 30 years, starting with the Shiny Brite bulbs I remembered from my childhood. I would often find them at flea markets for $1 a box.

Through the years, I have watched the prices of these machine-blown glass ornaments skyrocket. Selling them on eBay has been lucrative, as well as enjoyable, for me.

Several vintage ornaments made in Germany are part of my collection. These brightly colored ornaments are very thin glass and terribly fragile.

I also have a number of Shiny Brites in their original boxes, which are as hard to find as the ornaments themselves. Some of the World War II-era ornaments are "unsilvered," decorated with paint or small white mica crystals on the outside but no shiny coating inside.

Ornaments with paper caps are easy to date. They were made during WWII when metal could not be used.

I love collecting ornaments; it is a great hobby. I enjoy going to flea markets, and I never know what rarity I will come across.

WILLIAM OGDEN • WOOSTER, OH

SANTAS

KEEPING AN EYE OUT

I'm always looking for a different Santa for my collection. I have Santas from Italy, Poland and places I've gone on vacation. When I have family over, the children and parents love to pick out their favorites.

BETTY MOROZ • WARREN, MI

ELECTRIC LIGHTS

WHAT A TURN-ON!

A member of the Golden Glow of Christmas Past—an international collectors group—I save vintage GE lights and lighting guides.

JEFF CARTER • MABLETON, GA

ALUMINUM TREES

HOLIDAY OBSESSION

I've been preoccupied with vintage Christmas decorations ever since I bought an old Victorian home. I recently sold the house but packed up most of my decorations and more to move to a smaller abode.

I'm not sure if I'll be able to decorate like I did before. I once had nine trees. But I brought all of it with me anyway! One of my favorite trees is my 1950s aluminum tree that I decorate with pink Shiny Brite bulbs.

NANCIE BILLINGSLEY • TRAVERSE CITY, MI

BUBBLE LIGHTS

OLD-TIME GLOW

Collecting anything pre-1950s, especially bubble lights, is a pastime for my brothers Bud and Merle and me. Each of us has a Christmas room to display his stash. I try to imagine whose house items came from and who couldn't wait to see the last string of lights placed on the tree.

MIKE PALMER • KNOXVILLE, TN

10

HOLIDAY CANDLES

"

By the end of one antiquing weekend, my husband's collection, which had started with fewer than 10, was approaching 80 candles!

ROSEANN HILL • WHITAKER, PA

PREVIOUS SPREAD AND THIS SPREAD ORNAMENT BALLS 1-12: KAMENETSKIY KONSTANTIN/SHUTTERSTOCK; TINSEL TREE: ISTOCK.COM/PINK_COTTON_CANDY; BUBBLE LIGHTS: ETHAN DAVID KENT

BLOWN-GLASS FIGURES

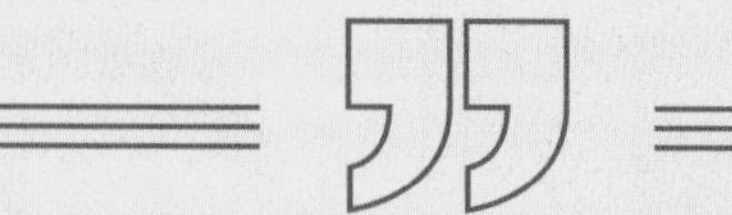

I have more than 600 glass ornaments. Some are over 100 years old. All of them are figural—no round balls.

NANCY NOWACZEK • GRAYSLAKE, IL

12 VINTAGE DECORATIONS

PAST BECOMES PRESENT

For many years I've been collecting vintage items from thrift stores—most things from the mid-20th century. My largest collection is of Christmas decor. When the holiday season begins, I turn my living and dining rooms into what I call "Santa's Thrift Shack on The Island of Misfit Ornaments."

MARY LYVERS CHISM • PENSACOLA, FL

FROM SHINY TO BRIGHT

Early Christmas tree decorations in America were often handmade, as store-bought glass or paper imports from Europe were expensive.

1920s

Until the mid-1920s, most imported blown-glass ornaments in the U.S. came from Germany.

1930s

When war in Europe threatened ornament supplies to the U.S. in the late 1930s, Max Eckardt, a German immigrant and ornament importer, persuaded Corning Glass Works of New York to modify its lightbulb-making machines and start producing glass ornaments.

Corning shipped its first mass-produced glass ornaments in December 1939 to Woolworth stores, where they sold for 2 to 10 cents each.

1940s

By the following year, Eckardt was using the Corning machinery to produce his trademark Shiny Brite ornaments: glass balls that were later silvered inside and hand-decorated and lacquered outside.

Material shortages during World War II forced design changes. Pastel-colored stripes on clear balls replaced shiny silvering and lacquer, and cardboard caps replaced metal ones.

Source: Bob Richter, *A Very Vintage Christmas*, 2016

BELL ORNAMENTS, SHINY BRITE BOXES: ETHAN DAVID KENT; ADS: NEIL BAYLIS/ALAMY STOCK PHOTO (3)

VINTAGE ADS

DEAR SANTA...

Adults and children alike delight in the gift-giving that surrounds the holidays. And marketers certainly never miss a beat!

1960

General Electric produced this ad featuring holiday gift ideas for the house. The headline plays off of the old-fashioned family shown.

An ad for shiny gifts from Toastmaster "...to show her she's a wonderful homemaker..." suggests that she'll be grateful.

1957

1957

In this holiday ad, Hoover doesn't imagine that anyone but the lady of the house will be doing the housework.

THE TIMELESS TINSEL TREE

The unusual tree that adorns my home every Christmas came from my grandparents Roscoe and Pauline Armentrout. It is from the late 1950s: an Evergleam Stainless Aluminum model that stands 6 feet tall and has 91 branches. When my mother cleaned out my grandparents' house, she shared memories of presents under the silver tree with me. I instantly fell in love with it and have used it in my home ever since. My grandmother is shown here with the tree in the 1960s.

REBECCA SIMPSON STEELE • BROOKLYN, NY